Wilbam J Fay

1. Inhereiting the Earth

Inheriting the Earth

BRENDAN BYRNE, SJ

Inheriting the Earth

The Pauline Basis of a Spirituality for Our Time

ALBA · HOUSE NEW · YORK

SOCIETY OF ST. PAUL, 2187 VICTORY BLVD., STATEN ISLAND, NY 10314

First published, September 1990 by ST PAUL PUBLICATIONS — Society of St. Paul, 60-70 Broughton Road — Homebush, NSW 2140.

Library of Congress Cataloging-in-Publication Data

Byrne, Brendan (Brendan J.)
Inheriting the earth : the Pauline basis of a spirituality for our time / Brendan Byrne.
p. cm.
Includes bibliographical references.
ISBN 0-8189-0603-0
1. Bible. N.T. Epistles of Paul — Theology. 2. Spirituality--Biblical teaching. I. Title.
BS2655.62B97 1991
227'.06 — dc20 91-9527
CIP

Designed, printed and bound in the United States of America by the Fathers and Brothers of the Society of St. Paul, 2187 Victory Boulevard, Staten Island, New York 10314, as part of their communications apostolate.

Printing Information:

Current Printing - first digit 1 2 3 4 5 6 7 8 9 10 11 12

Year of Current Printing - first year shown

1991 1992 1993 1994 1995 1996 1997 1998

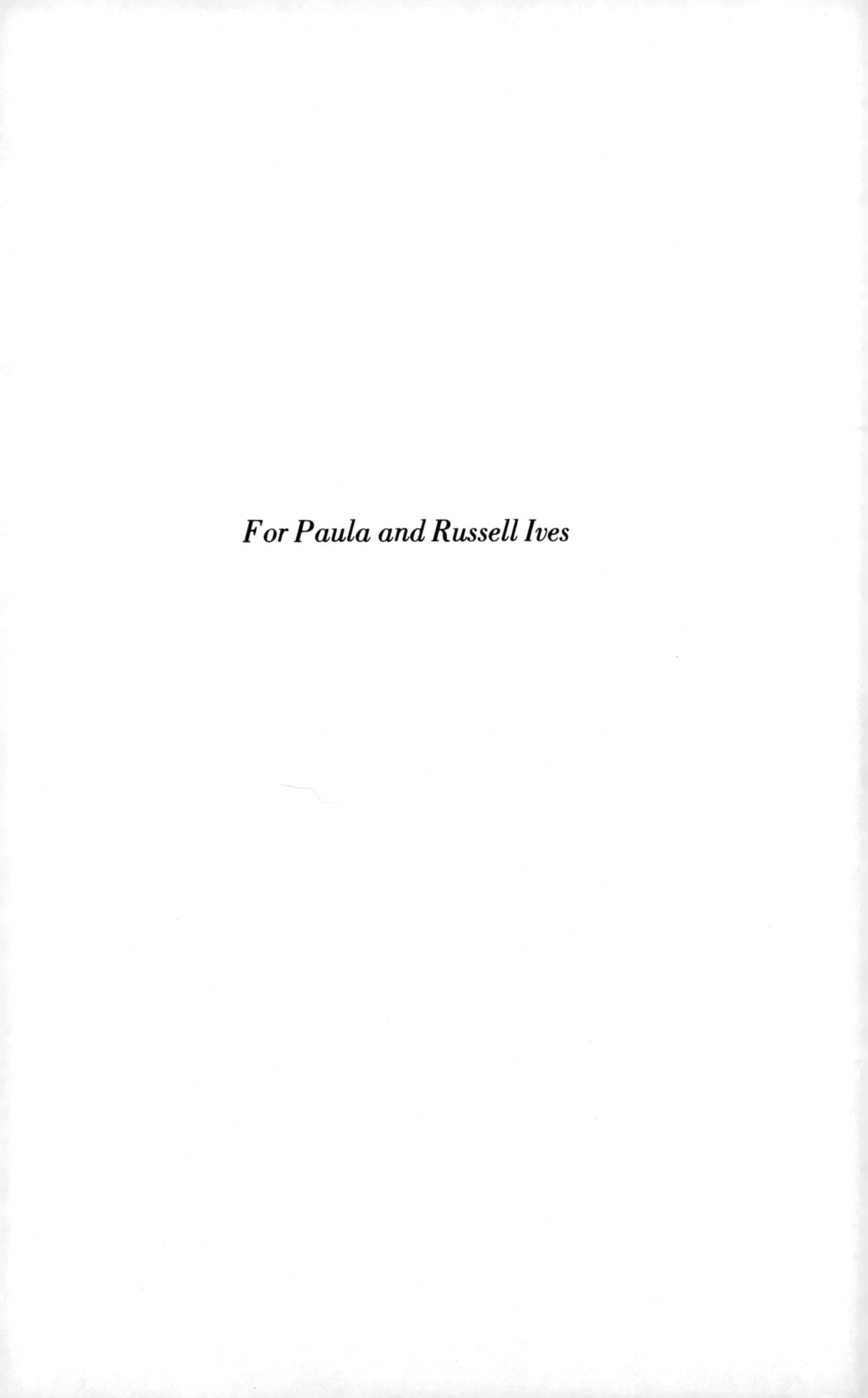

For Paula and Russell Ives

CONTENTS

INTRODUCTION

Two basic concerns stand behind the writing of this book. The first is the desire to make available to as wide an audience as possible an understanding of St. Paul valid for today. The second has to do with finding a spirituality that takes seriously the current concern for the fate of the world.

Many people familiar with Paul might regard this as a strange combination. Was not Paul's concern basically focused upon the community of believers — the proper order of the churches, the gaining of the Gentile world for Christ? Where in his writings do we find a concern for the earth? Did he not believe that the present world with all its structures was soon to pass away? How can one derive a "spirituality of the world" in the modern sense from Paul? All this is true. Yet I do believe Paul has much to say to our present concerns — just as he has spoken in different ways to Christians of preceding generations.

The voice of Paul was heard with renewed insistence in the sixteenth century at the time of the Reformation. Sadly, though, the recovery of the Pauline insights by the Reformers was not contained within the unity of the Church. And one unfortunate legacy of the Reformation quarrel was the tendency to see Paul as addressing very much the relationship between God and the individual believer. "How can I be justified?" "How can I be saved?" These were the questions that pressed heavily upon believers of that time.

But such an individualistic understanding is not really true to Paul and it is high time it was abandoned. In this book I hope to show that Paul founds a spirituality that is much more communal, one that is not concerned simply with the relationship between God and the individual Christian but bears essentially upon our life together and upon our world — what might be summed up as our total environment. More precisely, I want to insist that Paul, especially the Paul of the Letter to the Romans, points us directly to responsibility for the world as an integral part of our relationship with God. This means, among other things, that the insistence upon responsibility for the world that we find in Vatican II, especially in documents such as *The Church in the Modern World,* has a firm foundation in Paul.

My confidence that such is the case flows from a sense of the importance for Paul of the early chapters of the Bible (Genesis 1-3) where human responsibility for the world is a major element in the stories of creation. The first of these stories (Gn 1:1 - 2:4) describes the creation of human beings on the sixth day as the pinnacle of God's creative work (1:26-30). Made in God's own image and likeness, human beings are told to be fruitful and multiply, to fill the earth and subdue it and to have mastery over all other living things that move upon the earth (v. 28). This idea of creation in God's image and likeness played a central role in Paul's understanding of human existence. In particular, the vision of Genesis notably shaped his view of how God purposed to bring human beings and the world to the fullness of life through Christ. For Paul, Jesus is the "Adam" of the new creation, the one who successfully plays out the role which the first Adam disastrously muffed — the role of inaugurating a humanity that would live out the privilege and responsibility of being God's image in the world.

In making this claim, I fully realize that, whatever these stories of creation may have meant for Paul, there are many people today who look upon them with far less favorable eye. On the one hand, the inclusion of such creation accounts in "Holy Scripture" gives rise to attempts to defend and impose a strictly "creationist" view of the origin of the world and its forms of life. This remains a problem in circles where groups who do not accept that texts such as these teach religious rather than scientific truth have power in government and education. But it is not the only direction in which these stories can be misused. One can also question whether the Judeo-Christian idea of human mastery over creation has really worked for the benefit of the non-human rest of the world.

It cannot be denied that in many ways the "mastery" portrayed in Genesis 1-3 has been taken as an invitation more to exploitation and plunder than to responsibility. The fact that until recently at least the religious culture of Europe and North America has been Christian may have had little or much to do with the dominance in recent centuries of European technology and economic power. That can be argued back and forth. But the question must at least be faced as to how far an interpretation of a key foundational text has worked positively rather than negatively in human relating to the rest of the world.[1]

The use and misuse of the world in which we live has, of course, become a burning issue. As this century enters its last decade a whole new consciousness has spread across the world: a consciousness of global responsibility. For the first time it has struck home to millions, not just a select few, that human beings have the potential to ruin the earth, to effect changes that are irreversible, devastating in their consequences for all forms of life on our planet. The ruin might occur instantly through global nuclear exchange. It might come about more gradually through ecological decline. There is a new sense that, in either case, the fate of the race is at stake in that of the world. This consciousness transcends rivalries and barriers previously thought impenetrable — East-West, North-South. It translates itself into mass votes and movements of which even the most resistant political leaders are taking note. To be human in the 21st century is going to mean being conscious and caring for the earth in which we live — not just in the sense of one's own backyard or nation but the entire world. We now know that what is done — for good or ill — in one region vitally affects all. The spread of desert land in Africa does not leave Europe untouched; the Amazon rain forest is a resource not just for Brazil but for the globe.

Spirituality cannot neglect this concern and in recent decades has given it much attention. Most notable in this direction is the "creation spirituality" currently emanating from North America.[2] The present book is not inspired by nor strictly part of the "creation spirituality" movement. It shares the concerns of that movement and in many respects moves basically in the same direction. Like creation spirituality it will re-examine, in the light of Paul, certain emphases in the traditional view of redemption. It will do this in the hope that the doctrine of redemption might respond more directly to present human experience. I see no reason for clinging to models of redemption — or other theological tenets — which do not speak to our contemporary quest for God and which do not situate that quest in the context of what it means to be a member of the human race today. At the same time, seeking to present Paul's view, I shall not perhaps place as much stress on creation at the expense of the redeeming work of Jesus as creation spirituality appears to me to do.[3]

What I propose is, first of all, to "revisit," in the light of Paul, the Genesis accounts of creation. In particular, I should like to consider the vision of human existence that emerges from Genesis 1-3 and seems to have been foundational for Paul. This will place us in a position to trace Paul's reinterpretation of these texts and his understanding of them in the light of Christ and his own situation.

Key elements in this overall Pauline vision are: (1) Paul's sense of God as the faithful One, the Creator who takes ultimate responsibility for creation even when it wanders far away; (2) his view of the world as locked in a destructive, dehumanizing bondage to sin; (3) his sense of Christ as the obedient one who breaks the grip of sin, bringing new possibility and freedom; (4) his understanding of Christian existence as a being swept up into the costly faithfulness and responsibility for the world embodied in Christ; (5) his sense of hope for the future of the world that emerges from this view; (6) his view of "life in the body" as a life of belonging to a community which both celebrates and responsibly seeks under God's grace to enact and model this vision.

My sense is that by moving across these areas of Pauline thought we shall be able to build up a base for a spirituality that proceeds from Scripture and also speaks to the deepest needs of our time. That is, one which responds to the twin concerns I mentioned at the start.

I should perhaps add two more things concerning the method I propose to follow. First, the reflections will flow very largely, though not exclusively, from Paul's Letter to the Romans.[4] Readers familiar with that letter may detect that in many ways the sequence of topics appears to follow its order. This is no accident, nor does it need apology. Romans, in all likelihood Paul's last surviving letter, provides the mature and tested exposition of his gospel. It is natural that this letter should dominate any comprehensive exposition of his thought.

Secondly, in the matter of interpretation, particularly in the area of human responsibility for the world, I am well aware that I am going well beyond the limits of what Paul actually had in mind when he wrote to Rome. The late 20th century concerns sketched above hardly entered his imagination. But my interpretation of Paul stems from a belief, widespread in current interpretation, that the meaning of a text cannot be limited strictly or solely to what the author, ancient or modern, had in mind to say. The text once free from the author's hands gains a life and meaning of its own. The first readers and all who follow enter actively into the process of interpretation. The point I would wish to make in this respect is that, though my interpretation goes beyond Paul, it *extends his thought in the direction in which it is already moving.* In this sense I trust it may claim to be a legitimate interpretation, one entitled to speak in Paul's name to readers of his words today.

FOOTNOTES

1. The negative view of the influence of the Christian tradition on the environment found classic expression in a lecture, "The Historical Roots of our Ecological Crisis," delivered in 1966 by the American historian, Lynn White. This view has not gone unchallenged. For further references and a resume of the discussion see S. MacDonagh, *To Care for the Earth* (London: Chapman, 1986) 136-42.
2. Chiefly associated with Thomas Berry and Matthew Fox: see A. Lonergan & C. Richards, *Thomas Berry and the New Cosmology* (Mystic, CT: Twenty-Third Publications, 1987); M. Fox, *Original Blessing: A Primer in Creation Spirituality* (Santa Fe, NM: Bear & Company, 1983); idem, *The Coming of the Cosmic Christ* (New York: Harper & Row, 1988). For a resume and critique of "creation spirituality" see T.E. Clarke, S.J., "Theological Trends: Creational Spirituality," *Way* 29/1 (January 1989) 68-80.
3. My sense is that more emphasis on redemption is to be found in Matthew Fox's most recent book, *The Coming of the Cosmic Christ* (see previous note).
4. For a fuller exposition of the interpretation of Romans presupposed in this book I would refer the reader to my extended reading of the letter in quasi-commentary form: *Reckoning with Romans* (Good News Studies 18: Wilmington: Glazier, 1986).

Inheriting the Earth

1.

GENESIS REVISITED

The opening chapters of the Bible establish the attitude to the world characteristic of the Jewish-Christian tradition. Within the flow of that tradition the figure of Paul looms large. He inherits the ancient traditions of creation and reinterprets them in the light of Christ. This reinterpretation breaks new ground. But there is genuine continuity between what Paul received and the new understanding he passes on. Before we consider his reading of the creation texts, let us recall what we have in Genesis 1-3 taken by itself.

The Creation stories of Genesis

In Genesis 1-3 there are, of course, two quite distinct accounts of creation. The first (1:1 - 2:4) tells of God's creation of the universe within the seven-day framework of the Jewish week crowned by the Sabbath. It asserts, first of all, that all things have been made by God and, secondly, that God has declared the whole creation to be "good." Let us be clear about this last point. The Hebrew word for "good" here (*tov*) does not mean simply "good" in a vague, general kind of way. It has also a more dynamic sense of "useful," purposeful. The whole of God's creation is good in the sense that it is fitted together and moving towards a desired goal. In much the same way we might admire a fine motor car and dub it good because we see that all its component parts are designed to convey people from one place to another with maximum comfort, safety and speed.

Creation, then, is good. The very first text in the Bible encases that belief irrevocably in the Judeo-Christian tradition. If there is evil, this does not stem from the nature of things, but from some other source. The crowning achievement of God's work according to this text is the creation of human beings on the sixth day. Let us recall the relevant sentences:

> Then God said, "Let us make man in our image, after our likeness; and let them have dominion over the fish of the sea, and over the birds of the air, and over the cattle, and over all the earth, and over every creeping thing that creeps upon the earth,"
>
> So God created man in his own image,
> in the image of God he created him;
> male and female he created them.
>
> And God blessed them, and God said to them, "Be fruitful and multiply, and fill the earth and subdue it; and have dominion over the fish of the sea and over the birds of the air and over every living thing that moves upon the earth" (1:26-28).

I should like to draw attention to two things in particular here: (1) The repeated statement that human beings are created *in the image and likeness of God.* (2) The giving to human beings of *dominion* over the rest of creation — an idea repeated later on, in chapter 9, in the context of the covenant made after the Flood between God, human beings and "every living creature" found upon the earth.

Psalm 8 presents a similar view of human dignity in more poetic form:

> When I see the heavens, the work of your hands,
> the moon and the stars which you arranged,
> what is man that you should keep him in mind,
> mortal man that you care for him?
> Yet you have made him little less than a god,
> with glory and honor you crowned him,
> gave him power over the works of your hand,
> put all things under his feet (Ps 8:4-7).[1]

From this view of creation two central truths emerge:

1. Created in God's image, human beings are able to relate to God, to enter a relationship of interpersonal communion and intimacy. This is not just an incidental feature of human nature: relating to God enters essentially into the structure of human existence; it is a condition of life and death. In vital relationship to God human beings flourish; when the relationship breaks down, they wither and die.

2. Being in God's image also means relationship to the rest of creation. Before the gates of cities in the ancient world it was customary to erect an image or statue of the ruler. The image let all travellers entering the city know that they were coming under this ruler's writ and law. The motif in Genesis 1:26-28 of human beings created in God's likeness reflects this practice. Human beings image the Creator before the rest of creation. They are viceroys, as it were, exercising dominion in the Creator's name. The dominion is not one of selfish exploitation. The aim is to further the goodness, order and development of the world, to bring it to full achievement of its goal through respect for the sovereignty of God.

This is the biblical vision emerging out of Genesis 1. It suggests that the way human beings relate to the world and accept responsibility for it, enters essentially into their relationship with God.

With the second account of creation (2:5-25) we enter a

different world. The first human pair are now real characters — "the man" (*Adam* in Hebrew) and "the woman" (*Eve*) — and their separate creation (2:7, 21-23) is told in the form of a story. The world in which God places them is a garden. It is a delight, but also a responsibility: theirs to till and keep (2:15-16).

Only in one respect is there restriction. From the fruits of all trees may they eat save that of the tree of the knowledge of good and evil (2:17). Within the literary form of the story this command is not an arbitrary test of obedience. It is a symbol of general creaturely dependence upon God and trust in the Creator's good intentions. It does not detract from the sense of intimacy that pervades the account. The man and the woman enjoy a truly adult relationship with God.

And the same intimacy prevails in their relations with one another. They wear no clothes and are unashamed. In more psychological terms, they need no masks.

In chapter 3 a malign influence enters in. The serpent exploits the command by suggesting a false interpretation of God's purpose. God was trying to keep something back from human beings — a knowledge that would make them "like gods, knowing good and evil" (3:5). Within the frame-work of the total narrative (Genesis 1-3), they were, of course, already "like God" (1:26-28). Creaturely status came no higher than that. But the serpent turned their attention from their true dignity, sowing mistrust, delusion and ultimately rebellion against God. The core tactic was deception: a leading of human beings into the paths of death through a false promise of life where life was not to be found.

Once the couple succumb to the serpent's suggestion, the whole atmosphere changes. The intimacy with God is changed to fear; the adult relationship, lost. Conscious of their sin, the couple run away from God and hide like naughty children (3:8). The intimacy with one another yields to domination, blaming and accusation (3:12-16). And the relationship with the earth is also affected: it becomes barren, hard to till, yielding its fruits only through the sweat of human labor (3:17-19). So the break-down of relationship with God has meant the breakdown of relationships in all directions — including that of the relationship to the earth.

We do not read these creation traditions as "history" in any true sense of the word. Nor do we look to them to provide a scientific account of the origins of human beings or the wider world. Telling "how it all began" in poetry and story, they communicate a certain vision of human life and destiny. Central to that vision, as I have argued, is the sense of human beings in relationship both to God and to the rest of creation. And the relationships in both directions are bound up in such a way that damage to the one inevitably redounds ruinously upon the other. We shall see how strongly this "linkage" features in the thought of Paul.

Paul's view of the Genesis traditions

Paul not only reads Scripture (the Old Testament) in the light of Christ. He constantly finds Christ "back there" in the great events of Israel's past. The most striking instance of this is perhaps the way he identifies the "rock" that followed the Israelite camp in the desert simply and baldly with Christ: "and the Rock was Christ" (1 Cor 10:4). Paul can make such identification because he cannot see God giving life and guidance to human beings apart from Christ.

For Paul, however, Scripture is not really about "back there" at all — or at least not wholly so. Scripture speaks about God's communication of life now. Thus for Paul the biblical creation stories are not, as they can tend to be for us, instruction about the origin of the world and of human life. They tell of the "new creation" God is bringing about in Christ, proclaimed in the gospel. It is not so much that Jesus was at work "back there." Rather, the story which seems to be about what happened "back there" is really the story of what God has been accomplishing all along through Jesus Christ.

Within this overall approach to Scripture, Paul reads the early chapters of Genesis in a way that blends the two accounts of creation. Following a Jewish tradition, he sees the creation of the first man, Adam, already described in Genesis 1:26-28. Thus Adam is created in the image and likeness of God and given the mastery of the rest of creation described in that text.

But Paul's whole view of Adam is colored by what happens in chapter 3. His reading of the Genesis story is very pessimistic as far as Adam is concerned. Not only does Adam sin in himself, he initiates the sin-history of the whole human race. Paul sees in him not simply the first sinner, but the archetypal sinner — one who sets the pattern that all subsequent sinning will follow.

So in Paul's view Adam becomes the symbol of broken relationship with God. The story of his sinning prefigures the evil consequences that all human sinfulness entails: alienation in all relationships — from God, from fellow human beings, from the world — and a destiny to death. Adam tarnishes the image of God in which he has been made. He forfeits or, rather, misuses the dominion over the universe conferred upon him. He symbolizes all that goes wrong when human beings rebel against God.

But Genesis provides Paul with another story to set alongside this pessimistic "Adam" one. If he sees in Adam the symbol of broken relationship with God, the one in whom all consequent ills have their source, Christ is for Paul both the symbol of that relationship renewed and the facilitator of all the new possibilities opened up thereby. The following passage sets the two "stories" most clearly side by side:

Adam	*Christ*
[17]For if, through one man's trespass, death reigned through that one man	much more will those who accept the overflow of grace and the gift of righteousness reign in life through the one man, Jesus Christ.
[18]Therefore, as one man's trespass led to condemnation for all,	so also one man's act of justice leads to freedom and life for all.
[19]As through the one man's disobedience many were made sinners,	so through one man's obedience many will be found righteous.

[20](The law came in only to multiply the trespass. But where sin increased, grace abounded all the more.)

[21]So that, as sin reigned in death,	grace also might reign through righteousness for eternal life, through Christ Jesus, our Lord. (Rm 5:17-21 [author's translation])

Paul views Christ in "Adam" terms because he sees him reversing all that Adam has done. If "in Adam" one can read the story of human beings severing relationship with God and seeking the path of death, "in Christ" one reads the story of God offering renewal of relationship and possibility of life. If Adam symbolizes the ruin of God's designs for human beings, Christ is both symbol and enabler of their coming true.

Of course, if we look closely at this text we will see that Paul is not simply comparing side by side the "careers," so to speak, of Adam and Christ. He is asserting strongly the superior force of grace. If death reigned through Adam, *much more* will those who accept the gift of grace "reign in life through the one man, Jesus Christ" (v. 17). "Where sin increased, grace *abounded all the more*" (v. 20b). Adam simply represents human beings going it alone over against God. Behind the "Last Adam" (Christ) stands the power and presence of God. In the original creation, God triumphed over the chaos and the darkness (Gn 1:1-5). The victory will take place even more forcefully in the new.

This sense of the superiority of grace is important for the spirituality we should draw from Paul and we shall return to it in due course. For the present there is one other aspect of Paul's view of Christ in "Adam" terms that we should not overlook: Paul's sense of Christ as "image" or bearer of the glory of God.

When Paul speaks of Christ as "image" of God (2 Cor 4:4), as bearing upon his face the glory of the Creator (v. 6), he is really seeing him in terms of Genesis 1:26-28. The Risen Lord replays the "image" role that Adam failed. He perfectly "images" God before the new creation. This is why Paul can describe Christian conversion in these striking words: "the God who said, 'Let light shine out of darkness' (that is, the Creator God) has shone in our hearts to give the light of the knowledge of the glory of God in the face of Christ" (2 Cor 4:6).

Not only does the Risen Lord image God. He has also come into the possession of the universe that bearing God's image entails. It is as "image of God" that he is acclaimed as "Lord" by all creation (Ph 2:9-11). As such he "must reign until he has put all his enemies under his feet" (1 Cor 15:25, alluding to Ps 8:6). In short, the messianic rule which Christ begins at his resurrection is nothing other than that dominion over the universe which God intended for the human race from the start.

In Paul's view, then, this role of universal dominion

belongs first and foremost to the New Adam, Christ alone. Human beings regain or come into this privilege only in so far as they become one with the Risen Lord or, as Paul puts it, "are changed into his image." The change comes about as they enter and begin to live a life of faith. Paul sums it up in one of his most splendid sentences: "And we all, with unveiled face, seeing as in a mirror the glory of the Lord are being changed into his image from one degree of glory to another; and this comes from the Lord who is Spirit" (2 Cor 3:18).

So Paul sees Christ as "Last Adam," the "patriarch" in whom God founds a new humanity. In union with him and patterned after his mode of existence believers come into that possession of the universe that God intended for human beings from the start. This vision underlies the high claims Paul often makes for Christian existence:

> For all things are yours:
> whether Paul or Apollos or Cephas
> or the world or life or death or the present or the future,
> all are yours,
> and you are Christ's
> and Christ is God's.

These words to the Corinthians (1 Cor 3:21b-23), for all their ring of extravagance and exaggeration, express his sense of the original creative design coming true in Christ.

Two "stories" — two "ages"

So when Paul reads the Genesis text he finds it telling two "stories": a "sin-failure-death" story told in Adam and a "grace-success-life" story told in Christ. He casts these within the framework of a way of looking at salvation history inherited from the Jewish tradition of his day: the doctrine of the "Two Ages." This schema distinguished the present age or epoch sharply from an age to come. The present age — basically the current state of the world as viewed by the faithful community — was marked by sin, suffering and death. It was, in effect, evil beyond redemption. No hope for improvement could be expected save as a result of a cataclysmic intervention of God. This intervention would swiftly wind up the Present Age, with its authorities and rulers marked out for destruction. There would follow the New Age, the remaking, in effect, of the whole creation. In this new and final era the original design of the Creator for the human race and the world would come true for the first time. [2]

Paul, as I said, inherited this view from the Jewish tradition in which he was nurtured. However, for him as a Christian the doctrine of the "Two Ages," as it was known, underwent substantial modification. As noted above, the Jewish tradition distinguished sharply between the two Ages and held that God's intervention, though very close, was not yet at hand. Christians, on the other hand, saw the life, death and resurrection of Jesus as the beginning of the long awaited intervention of God. The Old (or Present), evil Age was still around; the New had not come in its entirety. But there was an overlap, an interpenetration between them. Believers still suffered, died and wrestled with the power of sin. But at the same time they viewed Christ's resurrection as the dawning of the new creation and felt in the Spirit its ongoing, life-giving force. The Spirit, welling up within, impelled them to cry out with Jesus, "*Abba*, Father" (Gal 4:6; Rm 8:15). In that address to God, characteristic of Jesus and of him alone, the intimacy of the first creation found echo and regeneration.

This sense of living "in the overlap" between the Ages stands at the heart of Paul's view of Christian life. It is a life in which one feels the tug of both Ages pulling in opposite directions: what Paul in his own terms describes as the choice between living "according to the flesh" (that is, the life of the Old Age) or "according to the Spirit" (that of the New). This choice, continually exercised, lies at the heart of any spirituality that claims inspiration from Paul.

We shall go more deeply into this matter of flesh and spirit later on. For the present I simply wish to indicate how Paul's sense of the "two stories," that told in Adam and that told in Christ, fits into and indeed flows from this doctrine of the Two Ages. The "overlap" or interpenetration of the ages means that both "stories" run in every human life, in every human situation.

The reason that Paul's message is "gospel" — *good* news — is that ultimately the "weighting," the prevailing power, lies with the grace of Christ. Paul's sense of hope is rooted in his vision of God as the Creator ultimately faithful to creation, even when creation has not itself kept faith. We shall move now to take up this view which enshrines his dominant view of God. But, following to some extent the pattern set out in Romans, I propose first of all to look more closely into the "Adam" story — to examine Paul's diagnosis of humanity gone wrong, the situation that calls forth the intervention, through Jesus Christ, of a gracious, faithful God.

FOOTNOTES

1. The Grail Translation: *The Psalms: A New Translation* (London: Collins, 1965) p. 20 used with permission of A.P. Watt Ltd. on behalf of The Grail, England.
2. My use of the phrase "New Age" here reflects an established scholarly usage based upon the distinction in ancient Jewish eschatology between the "this (present) age" and the "age to come." It is quite separate from the contemporary usage of "New Age" to describe a widespread philosophy or movement promoting a variety of emphases and techniques centering upon personal growth, heightened consciousness, unity with the cosmos, bio-feedback and so forth.

2.

THE PLIGHT OF THE WORLD

The Christian religion has a lot to say about sin. Yet many people might feel that, for all its concern about wrong-doing, Christianity fails to address real evil in the world. It is not that people today have lost a sense of sin. It is more that the sense of sin has undergone a change. People seem less inclined to catalogue, lament and seek forgiveness for individual sins — to set about the periodic rubbing-clean of the slate from all that has accumulated. Instead, they want to come to grips with a more deep-seated and abiding illness, something that holds their lives in a rut, poisoning relations with God and their fellow human beings. They sense that what are customarily called "sins" are really symptoms of a deeper malaise and that forgiveness must address this basic level if it is to be lasting and effective in their lives.

On a wider scale people have a sense of a world trapped in irresolvable conflict. We live under the threat of global destruction from a widespread pattern of sources — the arms race with its stockpiles of nuclear weapons, over-population, climatic and environmental breakdown, intolerable imbalance between North and South in terms of social and economic development, the devastation of AIDS. The whole world, which thanks to modern technology and communication could provide so pleasant an environment for all human beings, seems to be locked in a vise of suspicion, greed and noncooperation.

This for many people today is sin. Or, rather, this plight of the world is the effect of some mysterious deep-seated ill that might be termed radical sin. What people long for above all is not simply forgiveness of individual sins but liberation from this all-enveloping bind which strikes so devastatingly at the possibility of being human today.

Paul's sense of sin

What we find in Paul fits rather closely this modern sense of sin. Paul is not very interested in sins. True, alongside virtues to be embraced, he can list for his communities long lists of vices to be avoided (e.g., Gal 5:19-21, 22-23). He issues warnings about sinful behavior in specific areas — community life, sexual relations, social obligation. But such things for Paul are really symptoms of a more basic ill. To curb them is not really to address the root problem. When he speaks out of the gospel's heart Paul is always intent upon reaching for the core or nub of sin, the basic virus underlying all the symptoms. This radical quality of the analysis, together with the sense of a global bind "under" (the power of) Sin, is what gives Paul's understanding its power and penetration for today. Let us look more closely at Paul's radical sense of sin.

Central to Paul's Christian vision, as we have seen, is the idea of human beings created in God's image. Human existence is inconceivable except in relation to the Creator. For Paul, then, sin is basically that which comes in from the human side to poison and frustrate that relationship. It is an attitude first of suspicion, then of hostility to the Creator — a refusal to be a creature, to understand oneself as gifted rather than owed something by God. It is self-exaltation on the basis of a lie, a grasp for life independent of the One who alone sustains it.

I have said that Paul tends to speak of "Sin" rather than "sins." He personifies Sin, picturing it as a tyrant power that seeks to get human beings in its grip so as to alienate them from God and work its destructive effects. This view of Sin stems largely from Paul's reading of the "Fall" story in Genesis 3. In effect, he sees Sin cast in the role of the serpent in that story:

> . . . if it had not been for the law, I should not have known sin. I should not have known what it is to covet if the law had not said, "You shall not covet." But sin, finding opportunity in the commandment, wrought in me all kinds of covetousness. Apart from the law sin lies dead. I was once alive apart from the law, but when the commandment came, sin revived and I died; the very commandment which promised life proved to be death to me. For sin, finding opportunity in the commandment, deceived me and by it killed me (Rm 7:7b-11).

The commandment given to Adam not to eat of the fruit of a particular tree was basically, as we have seen, a symbol of human creatureliness before God. Paul adopts this understanding in the sense that he sees the specific prohibition as ruling out "covetousness" of any kind. He understands "covetousness" to embrace all the ways in which human beings seek to grasp independence over against God. The serpent in the "Fall" story used the commandment deceptively precisely to conjure up rebellion and mistrust: "You will not die . . . God knows that when you eat of it (the tree) your eyes will be opened and you will be like God, knowing good and evil" (Gn 3:4-5).

So Paul pictures Sin playing upon a basic human tendency to self-doubt, to question the value of simply being human before God, to disbelieve the immense dignity that flows from being made in the image of God, sharing life, communion and responsibility with the Creator. Sin preys upon an anxiety about littleness — an anxiety that seeks to compensate by self-assertion and independence, a desire for life over against rather than in communion with God.

In more psychological terms, sin for Paul entails a rampant and infectious selfishness. It rests upon the lie that "I" and not God stand at the focus of creation. It incites me to take all other creatures — "holy" and "religious" things included — and fit them into the project by which I try to build up my life. This is basically an attitude of *exploitation*. It sits in stark contrast to what might be called an attitude of *contemplation*, one that respects the autonomy of all other creatures and employs them reverently within the overall relationship to God. Over against a contemplative attitude to life (which is far from being a purely passive affair) sin poisons human relationships in all directions: it fractures the life-giving intimacy with the Creator and redounds ruinously upon my relationship with the rest of creation, human and non-human alike.

In this view the remedy required for sin is not primarily forgiveness. Paul does, it is true, adopt the early Christian view that saw Christ's death as expiatory sacrifice for sin (Rm 3:24-25). But God's willingness to forgive is something he tends to presuppose. Sin for Paul is not so much an offence that God must pardon, but a bind, a subtle enslavement from which human beings are set free in Christ. The issue is not forgiveness so much as liberation.

Sin and the plight of the world

Within this basic understanding of sin as enslaving power, Paul also powerfully depicts its destructive role in human relating to the world. A passage early in Romans sheds much light in this area. In Romans 1:18-32 Paul outlines the alienation of the Gentile (that is, non-Jewish) world from God. He wants to describe what happens when human beings break relationship with God and remain fixed in that alienation. What we read here is, of course, only a foil, a backdrop against which Paul will later (3:21-26) describe God's saving intervention in Christ. But, negative and somewhat disconcerting though it is, the passage pin-points both the core of sin and its wider destructive effects.

> [18]For the wrath of God is revealed from heaven against all the ungodliness and wickedness of men who by their wickedness suppress the truth. [19]For what can be known about God is plain to them, because God has shown it to them. [20]Ever since the creation of the world his invisible nature, namely, his eternal power and deity, has been clearly perceived in the things that have been made. So they are without excuse; [21]for although they knew God *they did not honor him as God or give thanks to him, but they became futile in their thinking and their senseless minds were darkened.* [22]*Claiming to be wise, they became fools,* [23]*and exchanged the glory of the immortal God for images resembling mortal man or birds or animals or reptiles.*
>
> [24]Therefore *God gave them up* in the lusts of their hearts to impurity, to the dishonoring of their bodies among themselves, [25]because *they exchanged the truth about God for a lie and worshipped and served the creature rather than the Creator,* who is blessed for ever! Amen.
>
> [26]For this reason *God gave them up* to dishonorable passions. Their women exchanged natural relations for unnatural, [27]and the men likewise gave up natural relations with women and were consumed

> with passion for one another, men committing shameless acts with men and receiving in their own persons the due penalty for their error.
> [28]And since *they did not see fit to acknowledge God, God gave them up* to a base mind and to improper conduct. [29]They were filled with all manner of wickedness, evil, covetousness, malice. Full of envy, murder, strife, deceit, malignity, they are gossips, [30]slanderers, haters of God, insolent, haughty, boastful, inventors of evil, disobedient to parents, [31]foolish, faithless, heartless, ruthless. [32]Though they know God's decree that those who do such things deserve to die, they not only do them but approve those who practice them.

This is hardly an attractive passage. Encountering it early in Romans deters many from reading further. If we look closely, however, we will soon grasp its essential role within Paul's wider purpose.

The passage has a clearly discernible structure. Three times there is a description of a fundamental refusal on the part of human beings to acknowledge God as Creator (vv. 21-23; v. 25; v. 28); three times we encounter the curious expression "God gave them up" (v. 24; v. 26; v. 28); three times there follows — in increasingly lurid detail and with heavy emphasis on sexual deviation — a description of the disastrous effects in human life of the break in relations with God.

This somewhat artificial structure of the passage suggests that it had a history prior to its appearance in Paul's letter to Rome. In fact, Paul seems to have adapted for his own purposes a Jewish tract against the idolatry of the pagan world rather similar to what we find in the Book of Wisdom (chapters 13-15).

But neither idolatry nor sexual deviation is Paul's central

concern. Rather, where the tract railed against idolatry, Paul takes it up because he wants to present idolatry as a paradigm of the core or essence of sin — as illustrative of the basic sin from which all evil flows. The tract depicted the vices of the pagan world as flowing from the fundamental rupture with the Creator that idolatry entails. In this it served well Paul's purpose to depict all other sins and social disorder as flowing from what he believed to be the core and nub of sin.

Paul's adoption of the tract places him within a long-standing Jewish tradition of revulsion at the sexual mores of the Greco-Roman pagan world. Homosexual practice, in particular pederasty, was seen as typical of the depravity of that world and linked specifically to the religious deviation represented by idolatry. Neither the Jewish tradition nor Paul made the modern distinction between homosexuality as a (pre-moral) psychological orientation and homosexuality as a chosen pattern of behavior. The passage cannot be seen in a simplistic way as providing blanket biblical condemnation of sexual deviance. Paul does not in fact use the tract to target specific vices against which he wants to warn the Christians of Rome; he leaves instruction on Christian behavior, as is his custom, to the closing part of the letter (chapters 12-15). Rather, the account of moral degeneracy here serves graphically to illustrate the lostness and depravity of the surrounding pagan world. The vices, the "sins" are the symptoms of the underlying fundamental break with God. For Paul they constitute a "revelation" of the "wrath" or anger of God (v. 18).

God's "wrath" in Paul's understanding does not really denote an emotion in the Creator. Following a biblical tradition Paul sees God's wrath as the *situation* that comes about when human beings opt out of relationship with God and are left for a time in the plight that then follows. It is not that God in anger rains down punishment. God does not add to the evil in the world by making fresh trouble. That is not Paul's view of God.

What punishment there is comes out of the situation — sin turns into its own punishment. By talking of the "revelation" of God's wrath Paul is saying, "Look, this is what happens when human beings turn away from relationship with God and are left for a time helplessly in that situation." They become trapped in their own wrongdoing. Relationships deteriorate in all directions — relationships with their own bodies, within the family, society, the world. The alienation from God results in an alienation that is truly universal.

I said above that three times this passage describes the process of alienation. Basically the second description (v. 25), "because they worshipped the creature rather than the Creator," sums it up. But it is worth dwelling a little longer on the first account that comes to a head in verse 23. We have to read it in the light of the first creation story in Genesis 1. The good things of God's creation should lead human beings to gratitude and praise of the Creator (v. 20). Instead of going through to the Creator, they have stopped short at the created world and given to mere creatures the honor and glory due to God alone (v. 21).

Notice, again, the element of deception in this account: "Claiming to be wise, they became fools" (v. 22). It is the story of Genesis 3 all over again (though the language actually owes much to the Greek version of the allusion in Ps 105:20 to the account of Israel's apostasy in the episode of the golden calf Ex 32:1-6). Human beings are deluded into thinking that through giving themselves to items of the created world in a worshipful way they will gain power and mastery. They forget that that mastery is already theirs — in a benign sense — through their being created in the image and likeness of God. They end up enslaved by that which they sought to master and become set on the path to death. As verse 23 puts it, "they exchanged the glory of the immortal God for images resembling mortal man or birds or animals or reptiles" (v. 23). That is, they "exchanged" the dignity that was theirs, their being made "in the image and likeness of God," for the indignity of a likeness to brute beasts. From being "God-like" they became "like" beasts — destined to die forever.

The presupposition behind all this is that God is the only being to whom you can give yourself totally and be set free. If you give yourself to anything less than God with that totality of giving that worship demands, it will enslave you. Idolatry of any kind leads to enslavement. That is the fundamental principle of Paul, following the biblical and Jewish tradition.

As we noted above, idolatry as such, in the sense of pagan worship, is not Paul's main concern in Romans. Rather he is letting idolatry serve as a paradigm of all sin or, rather, of the core or heart of sin. At base for Paul sin is idolatry because it consists in human refusal to let God be Creator and to be oneself simply creature — in dignity and trust — before God.

Even less than Paul are we concerned with idolatry. But we can write in the idols of our own age — idols from which we seek mastery and a promise of life that turns into illusion: drugs, nuclear weapons, financial manipulation, and so forth. The genius of Paul's account is that it goes beneath the symptoms to uncover the fundamental alienation.

At the same time the passage shows how the break with God brings alienation in every other direction. Sin is not merely a private problem between God and the individual. The rest of creation essentially enters in. Sin disrupts the whole pattern established in creation and redounds ruinously upon society and the entire created world. In this it leads to dehumanization since human beings can only be truly human when properly related both to Creator and creation. They flourish only in right relationship to the world in which they are creatively active. To ignore the world on the one hand, to be absorbed by it on the other, is delusion. Sin is ultimately a refusal to take responsibility — or, rather, to share, be caught up in the responsibility of the Creator.

My sense is that this analysis of sin, inherited by Paul from Jewish reflection upon Genesis 1:26-27, has more rather than less validity at the present time. Since the late 1960's space travel has provided pictures and photographs of our world taken as a whole — a powerful symbol of "one world." Advance in communications and transport has made the sense of "global village" a reality. We now have the means to grasp imaginatively the extent of human responsibility for the fate of the world. This means that the "end of the world," once considered something *God* might bring about, is now a frightening human possibility — whether it comes about in one devastating blow through nuclear exchange or through the slower but equally fatal onset of environmental breakdown. The "wrath of God" is not something to be unleashed as end-of-time punishment for evil. Rather, as Paul puts it in Romans 1:18, the "wrath of God" *is being revealed* here and now as a result of human sin. The "wrath" is the devastation — moral and physical — that flows from human refusal to live in a way that is both creaturely and creative in the world. The eschaton, the "end of the world," which the more apocalyptic biblical writings assigned to the power of God, lies firmly in human hands. It is the result, rather than the punishment, of human sin.

In this reflection upon the wider implications of human sin I have, of course, gone well beyond the limits of Paul's own thought. But I would argue that his depiction of the revelation of God's "wrath" being realized in the personal and social devastation of the Gentile world (Rm 1:18-32) is beginning to move in this direction. His view of God's wrath already being revealed challenges the idea that human sin simply stokes up divine punishment at some future day of reckoning. God does not add to the sum of evil by introducing fresh punishment for sin. The "punishment" issues from within the situation of a world where the "sin" story, rather than the "grace" story, has been allowed to run. Evil stems ultimately from the fundamental human refusal to acknowledge God as God and the world as the field of human responsibility before the Creator.

"Insider" sin

Paul makes one further move in his analysis of the plight of the world "under" sin. If the power of sin can show itself in the form of the dehumanizing vices to be seen in the surrounding world, it can also work an equal destructiveness in those who would consider themselves on the "inside" as far as moral uprightness and God's favor is concerned. Following the passage we have just considered Paul turns upon one whom he calls the "judger" (Rm 2:1). At first he does not reveal who he has in mind. But eventually it becomes clear that his indictment of the Gentile world is being followed by a warning to the Jews. Conscious of their favored status as God's chosen people and the undoubted moral advantages they enjoy through possession of the law, they are prone to complacency and presumption. They do not recognize that the power of sin can subtly undermine their relationship to God and place them in a situation of alienation akin to that of the Gentile world. Like the Elder Brother in Luke's parable of the Two Sons (15:11-32), they can so identify sin with the vices of the Gentile world (illustrated by the plight of the Younger Brother) that they can fail to see how sin can pervert their own relationship with God.

Paul is not here making an empirical judgment upon the life of his Jewish brethren. Above all he is not formulating an accusation valid against Jewish religion as such, then or now. He is simply inviting those who hear his gospel as "insiders," so to speak, to consider in the Spirit the subtle ways in which sin may infiltrate the recesses of their commitment to God. The temptation is always there to rest upon grace and a sense of privilege, to understand one's religious insight and knowledge as a guarantee of salvation over against the "other" who remains outside, to "thank the Lord that one is not as the rest of men" (the Pharisee in the parable of Luke 18:9-14).

Such an attitude gives rise to an individualistic quest for salvation that largely ignores the plight of the rest of the world or sees it as a field for the exercise of my personal virtue. Though outwardly good and holy, this quest is a manifestation of sin because it too ends up pursuing its own designs rather than surrendering in love and homage to the plan of the Creator. It fails to take seriously the responsibility for the entire world given to human beings according to Genesis 1:26-27. It sets limits around the holy, the acceptable; beyond these it will not move. When the well-intentioned scribe asked Jesus innocently, "Who is my neighbor?" (Lk 10:29-37), he hardly expected the "definition" which, in story form, he received. By indicating the despised Samaritan as the one who showed himself neighbor Jesus broke through the kind of limit imposed by a religious attitude such as this. He showed that neighborly concern must be worldwide in scope if it is not to fall under the limitation that Paul would ascribe to the subtle working of sin.

Paul can in fact say bluntly that "all that does not proceed from faith is sin" (Rm 14:23). We can see what he means when we understand that for him faith involves basically an acknowledgement of God as Creator and a willingness to surrender one's life project to God in obedience and loving trust. As such, faith is the very opposite of sin, which, as we have seen, consists basically in human desire to manage life independently of relationship with God.

Conclusion

What I have attempted to do here is to give some account of Paul's understanding of sin and his sense of its deep-seated working in human personal and social life. I have tried to make more explicit the allusions his analysis frequently makes to the traditions of Genesis 3 and to the figure of Adam in particular. "In Adam," as we have seen, Paul sees told the "sin story" of the human race, the unleashing of a legacy of sin and death that gathers momentum as human history unfolds. Paul's view is not, as some earlier writers believed, that all of us somehow sinned "in Adam" before we were born, inheriting thereby some aspect of his guilt. That view of "Original" Sin may be traditional, but it is not right on the basis of a mistranslation of Romans 5:12 to foist it on to Paul.[1] Paul speaks of "Sin" as a kind of enslaving power — a virulent contagion of human selfishness and hostility to God. By nominating Adam as the one who let Sin get a foothold in the human race and as the one whose career sets a pattern of sinful alienation for all generations to come, Paul asserts that there is a solidarity in human sinning which both precedes and influences every human life. No one sins entirely alone and no one sins without adding to the collective burden of the race and the plight of the world.

This is the "sin-story" Paul tells in Adam. Its realization in every age unleashes forces of death and destruction in the world. In religious terms it is fundamentally a story of alienation and broken relationship with God. Were it the only story Paul had to tell, his "gospel" would be bad news indeed. Over against it, however, he sets a "grace" story — one much more powerful and told "in Christ." Let us now turn to the positive face of the gospel for Paul.

FOOTNOTES

1. The mistranslation consisted of reading the final clause of Paul's sentence as "in whom all sinned" — the "whom" referring to Adam. This is certainly wrong. The "sinning" referred to here is the personal sinning of Adam's descendants in their own lives. It is difficult to give a simple literal translation of the Greek. In the latter part of the sentence Paul wants to say something like "and so sin passed to all on the basis that they followed Adam in his sin." For a fuller discussion of this interpretation see, B. Byrne, " 'The Type of the One to Come': Fate and Responsibility in Romans 5:12-21," *Australian Biblical Review* 36 (1988) 19-30, esp. pp. 25-27.

3.

CHRIST: THE FAITHFULNESS OF GOD

The New Testament expresses the one Christian faith in quite a variety of ways. This is something increasingly recognized in recent years. Each of the major documents views the life and death of Jesus in its own distinctive way. For Matthew he is the new Moses founding a community schooled in the kingdom of heaven. For Mark he is the Son of God, who in his obedience and suffering exorcises the evil of the world, bringing in the "kingdom" or "rule" of God. Luke likes to present Jesus as the great Prophet, bearer and communicator of the Spirit. John presents God's eternal Word, speaking on earth the life-giving revelation. For the author of Hebrews, Jesus is the High Priest of the new and surpassing covenant.

Within this range of New Testament Christology, we can say that for Paul Jesus is the one who embodies the saving faithfulness of God. The story of Christ, the "grace" story, is the story of the Creator faithful to creation. Once again, it is a story which begins in the Old Testament and there we must return to search out its origins in Israel's view of God.

A faithful God

"Saving faithfulness" translates a biblical term for which the older English translations tended to use "righteousness."[1]

"Righteousness" in the biblical sense refers to faithfulness within the demands of a relationship. Persons are dubbed righteous when within the terms of the relationship they are reckoned to have "done the right thing" by some other person or by society as a whole. So, in Israelite society, if I felt myself to have been unjustly treated by someone and a judge to whom I have had recourse awards a fair decision, I would proclaim that judge as "righteous." It does not mean that the judge is morally upright in every way. But precisely within the framework of the relationship with me as judge he has done the right thing by me. It is the sense of relationship that is crucial.

The Israelites thought of themselves as bound in relationship to the God who had rescued their fathers from Egypt, struck a covenant with them at Sinai and created them as a people. National life and well-being depended upon the proper working of this relationship. The faithfulness or righteousness of God underpinned the fabric of society and, indeed, the whole social and cosmic order.

God's faithfulness could be seen in all aspects of life. The Creator gave growth and fertility through the cycle of the seasons. If the rains came on time, if the harvest were plentiful, this showed fidelity to creation. Many psalms and other texts also hymn the faithfulness that gave victory and rescue in time of war. So the "righteousness" or faithfulness of God showed itself in *saving* acts. In the end, God's righteousness came to mean much the same thing as "salvation" (Is 45:8; 46:12-13; 51:5-6).

On the human side of the relationship a corresponding "righteousness" was required. The biblical record, however, shows that from the beginning this was hardly ever the case. Israel as a nation and key officials such as kings and judges rarely displayed full righteousness in social and religious spheres. False gods were worshipped; oppression of the poor and vulnerable was not restrained. Society did not reflect the "righteousness of God." The result was political and national ruin, as the prophets never ceased to proclaim. In fact we may say that the Old Testament as a whole is very much a documentation of the saving faithfulness of God in the face of human sin.

Here we strike upon something central to the biblical tradition. It might be thought that, if one partner of a contract defaults, the other is absolved from further obligation. But relations between God and Israel did not work that way. Israel's unfaithfulness and sin did not irrevocably break the relationship. The consequences of sin and infidelity may have been allowed to work themselves out for a time — sometimes with seemingly drastic and final results, as in the case of the Babylonian exile. But the same prophets who were unsparing in their proclamation of guilt and judgment also taught Israel to wait upon the ultimate faithfulness of God. God will do the right thing by Israel even if the nation has not done the right thing by God.

This is the central message of the unknown prophet of the Exile who speaks in Isaiah 40-66. The God who delivered Israel out of Egypt would bring about a new Exodus, return the Israelites to their homeland and restore the national life. Israel might not be deserving of such rescue. But God would act to show faithfulness and willingness to save. Precisely in the face of Israel's sin and desperate plight God would display saving power before the world. This is the "good news" or "gospel" which the "messenger to Zion" must announce (Is 40:9).

On a more personal scale, Psalm 143 expresses an appeal based on a similar confidence in the faithfulness and saving power of God. The psalmist, in desperate straits, admits to having no "righteousness" in God's sight. But at the beginning and the end of the prayer we hear a confident appeal to the faithfulness and righteousness of God:

[1]Hear my prayer, O Lord;
give ear to my supplications.
In your faithfulness answer me,
in your righteousness.
[2]Enter not into judgment with your servant, for no one living is righteous before you.
[The central verses describe the plight of the psalmist and beg for rescue]
[11]For your name's sake, O Lord, preserve my life!
In your righteousness bring me out of trouble!
[12]And in your steadfast love cut off my enemies, . . .
for I am your servant.
[RSV translation slightly altered]

We may note the way in which God's "righteousness" stands in parallel to similar ideas such as "faithfulness" and "steadfast love." We may note, too, how the appeal to righteousness at the beginning and the end "frames," as it were, all that stands between. The whole psalm is a beautiful act of confidence in the readiness and power of God to save precisely because Israel has a righteous God.

Paul: God faithful in Christ

This age-old biblical pattern where a faithful/righteous God confronts an unfaithful/unrighteous Israel flows directly into the theology of Paul. But now, under the influence of Isaiah 40-66, it undergoes broadening in a most notable way. The exilic prophet enlarged the scope of Israelite religion by proclaiming Israel's God to be Creator and Lord of the universe as a whole. The saving acts of God are played out on a universal, cosmic scale. Paul picks this up in the sense that he sees that what God is doing in Christ is exercising faithfulness as Creator not only to the Jewish people (Israel) but to the whole world as well. The gospel urges all people, Gentiles as well as Jews, to come under the scope of the saving action of God. Paul, of course, traces this universalist impulse back to God's promise to Abraham that "all nations" would be blessed "in his seed" (Galatians 3-4; Romans 4). But it is Isaiah's concept of the Creator faithful to creation that particularly governs his thought.

Moving from this Old Testament pattern, Paul presents Christ as the very embodiment of the saving righteousness of God. In Jesus' life, death and resurrection God has reached out to a lost, alienated world and freely offered renewal of relationship. The Creator has "done the right thing" by creation. That is why the gospel proclaims the "righteousness of God" (Rm 1:16-17). The whole argument of Romans runs along this line.

Christ, then, for Paul comes very much "from the side of God" — embodying the faithfulness of the Creator to a fallen world. But, as we noted earlier, Paul also thinks of Christ as the one who replays the role of Adam; he is the new first ancestor of the race. It is as a *human* being, not some visitor from an alien world, that Christ embodies the faithfulness of God. In his fidelity the divine and human axes intersect.

Central to Christian faith, however, is the sense that God's act of faithfulness in Christ confronts a world alienated by sin from its source of life. As Paul expresses matters in Romans 5:8: "What shows God's love for us is that it was while we were still sinners that Christ died for the ungodly." This state of affairs on the human side meant that renewal of relationship was not to be achieved without cost, a cost borne by Christ in his obedience "unto death, death on a cross" (Ph 2:8).

It is well, perhaps, that we should dwell for some time on the way Paul relates the costly aspect of Christ's work to the faithfulness of God. Some traditional ways of viewing the redemptive aspects of Christ's death bear reexamination in the light of fresh insights from the biblical background of Paul's thought.

Paul, it is true, uses the word "redemption" (Greek *apolutrôsis*) with respect to God's work in Christ (Rm 3:24). In the wider biblical tradition "redemption" has primarily the sense of being rescued and set free; it is used particularly in connection with Israel's liberation from slavery in Egypt. But the word can also set up overtones of a cost or price being paid. Also, along with a wider strain in early Christianity, Paul describes Christ's death in sacrificial and cultic terms. More particularly, in Romans 3:25-26 he alludes to the Jewish Day of Atonement, describing Christ's death as an expiatory sacrifice for sin. Let us examine more closely this text and the "Day of Atonement" ritual it appears to presuppose:

> God put him (Jesus) forward so that in the shedding of his blood he might be a means of expiation operative through faith. This took place to show God's righteousness with respect to all the sins passed over during the period of his patience and also with a view to showing his righteousness in the present time — so that he shows himself to be righteous precisely in his justifying a person through the faith of Jesus. [Author's translation]

Israel believed that on the Day of Atonement God renewed the covenant relationship by "wiping away" or "expiating" all the sins of the people that had accumulated over the past year. The high point of the ritual occurred when, following the prescription of Leviticus 16:15-16, the High Priest entered the Holy of Holies in the Temple and sprinkled the blood of a goat upon the cover (called in Greek *hilastêrion epithêma*) of the Ark of the Covenant. The rite, especially the sprinkling of the blood, did not serve to move or win the forgiveness of God. That was presupposed. The cultic act was the means by which God enacted and communicated to the people the promised purgation of sin and renewal of relationship. It enabled the people to be caught up within the saving act and feel its effects. The initiative remained entirely with God who had instituted both rite and priesthood in the first place.

Paul, in all likelihood relying upon an earlier Christian tradition, employs this sacrificial imagery in order to find meaning in the bloody death of Christ. He speaks of God "putting him (Jesus) forward so that in the shedding of his blood he might be a means of expiation (Greek *hilastêrion*) operative through faith." The use of such imagery follows an age-old human tendency to employ the language of sacrifice in an attempt to find meaning in the wastage of death. War memorials, epitaphs speak — perhaps less convincingly as the present war-stained century draws to its close — of those who made the "supreme sacrifice."

The problem, however, is that the image can develop a life of its own. It can become the dominant explanation of why the death in some way "had" to take place, why the sacrifice "had" to be offered.

This has certainly happened in the way later generations understood Paul. The biblical background to his "expiation" language was forgotten and the Greek term he uses — *hilastêrion* — was taken in its sense in everyday secular usage where it does refer to appeasing or placating an angry person or god. This gave rise to a view of redemption where the costly death of Christ was seen as necessary in order to assuage or placate God's righteous anger at human sin. Relationships between God and the human race were viewed within a tight sacrificial logic where God's love and forgiveness could not operate until costly satisfaction was paid in terms of the bloody death of Christ. We might recall the lines of a hymn often sung at

Easter: "That blessed Son who bought our peace and made his Father's anger cease" — a very poor translation of the fine Latin Sequence, *Victimae Paschali,* upon which it is meant to be based.

Though Paul's language in Romans 3:25-26 has undoubtedly led in this direction, such a view of redemption hardly responds to his broader understanding. The whole thrust of his thought emphasizes God's faithfulness and willingness to save. It is faithfulness which impels the Creator to reach out and restore relationship with an erring world. Christ is not a means of overcoming any blockage to forgiveness caused by anger at human sin. Christ works the renewal of relationship (justification) offered by a gracious God. In Paul, as in the Day of Atonement liturgy, the whole initiative stems from the side of God.

In this understanding the reason for Christ's death does not stem from some demand on God's side. The suffering is not a "cost" that must be paid to God. The cost arises out of the human situation. Christ suffered, not because God directly willed him to suffer and die, but because he embodied God's love, God's faithfulness in a world alienated from its Creator, a world where the "sin" story had set up encased structures of selfishness, self-interest and pride. That world struck back at Jesus because in his teaching, in the company he kept and the stances he took, he consistently represented perfect human response to the God of grace. This abiding responsiveness, rather than the following of a specific command, was what made up his obedience "unto death, even the death of a cross" (Ph 2:8).

It is in this sense that Paul sets the obedience of Christ over against the disobedience of Adam (Rm 5:19; cf. Ph 2:6-8). Son of God though he was, Christ modelled perfectly human creaturely relationship to God; creature though he was, Adam modelled the sinful human aspiration to be "as God." In

Adam is told the age-old story of human refusal to be a creature in love and responsibility before God. Christ facilitates and models the new possibility opened up by grace.

The passion of Jesus represents the moment where the two "stories," the "sin story" and the "grace story," came to the high point of conflict and where sin, for a time, seemed to gain the upper hand. The resurrection is God's assertion that the prevailing power lies with grace and with life. Nothing puts it better than two lines of the hymn just mentioned in its original Latin form:

> *Mors et vita duello conflixere mirando;*
> *Dux vitae mortuus regnat vivus.*
> [Death and life contended in a strange conflict;
> The Prince of life, once slain, now reigns alive.]

Model of redemption

Let us look a little more closely at the model of redemption that seems to emerge from this understanding of Paul's thought. We have tended to understand the redemption rather much in the following way. There was an original creation, a time of innocence in a paradise. Sin came in and there was a catastrophic fall from this original innocence. Then came the redemptive work of Jesus Christ, which *restored* the original situation. Here we have a sequence of stages, where one stage is over and complete before the next one comes in. The end result, what Christ achieves, is basically to restore the original situation.

I do not think this is precisely Paul's view of things. He does not see redemption so much in terms of stages, each following upon another already complete. Rather, the two "stories," the "Adam" story and the "Christ" story, are being told, are being verified in our world *at the same time*. That is, Adam and Christ present two possibilities for our world: a "sin," "death," "failure" story (Adam) and a "grace," "life," "success" story. And what God is doing in Christ is not so much restoring an original situation but allowing the original creative plan for human beings and the world to come true for the first time.

All examples limp, but this may help. Let us suppose that a group of families band together to form a commune in an idyllic country setting. They are inspired by an idea brought from an overseas country by the founder of similar settlements there. For a year or so all goes well — there is harmony, peace, bliss, in a beautiful natural setting. Then the harmony breaks down, the peaceful life is rudely disturbed, the continuing existence of the commune is threatened. An emissary comes from abroad to fix things up. He succeeds, at some cost, in restoring the original pattern — to the satisfaction of the founder overseas.

Now let us look at the history of the same commune from a rather different perspective. The community is there. Things may go well at first. But, looking at it, we can recognize that there are always two possibilities present: there is the possibility that the selfishness ingrained in human nature might come to the fore and lead to the destruction of the community; there is also the possibility that unselfishness (grace) might prevail, leading to a flourishing community life and individual personal growth. Here you do not so much see a sequence of stages — innocence: fall: restoration — but rather a continuing struggle to grow as individuals and as a community, where grace might win out over selfishness and so promote growth and life. At each moment of its existence the community is open to both possibilities.

This last, I think, is closer to the model Paul has in mind. The "Adam" story is not over and done with when Christ comes on the scene. Nor is it totally abolished through his redemptive work. It is still very much an actuality, a possibility in our lives and in our world. In what God has done in Christ is found the possibility for the other story to win through. The Creator has shown faithfulness by radically addressing in Christ the age-old blockage sin presents to the ongoing work of creation. This is the sense in which, for Paul, Christ embodies the saving faithfulness of God.

The death of Jesus, it is true, was a once-and-for-all historical event that cannot and need not be repeated. In raising the crucified, obedient One, God ensured the radical victory of grace. But till the end of time the conflict between grace and sin continues — in every individual human life, in every succeeding generation. The redemption strikes home, as it were, when human beings appropriate the victory of Christ in their lives and social context, when they allow the "grace" story told in Christ, rather than the "sin" story told in Adam, to have the upper hand.

Now that we have considered what God has done in Christ, it is time to turn to the side of human response, to consider what attitude makes it possible in Paul's eyes for the victory to lie with grace. How should human beings respond to the gospel so that in each succeeding generation the forces of life and true humanity rather than those of death and destructiveness prevail?

FOOTNOTES

1. The Catholic tradition, following the Latin, preferred to speak of "justice." Both traditions of translation had their disadvantages. "Righteousness" smacks of religious-biblical jargon, with little relevance to everyday life. "Justice" connotes principally the idea of fairness — and that is far from the biblical meaning. The New Jerusalem Bible speaks of "saving justice," a step in the right direction. Personally, I prefer to speak of "faithfulness" because I think that is the most central idea in Paul's usage.

4.

THE PRIORITY OF FAITH

Paul is, of course, well known as the great New Testament writer on faith. Such emphasis upon faith, however, might seem to undercut the purpose of this book. How can a spirituality of responsibility for the world be found in one who so stressed faith over against "works"? Must not Paul be opposed to an activist spirituality of any kind?

That Paul stressed faith *at the expense* of Christian behavior or responsibility is, of course, a caricature — a legacy of Reformation quarrels now largely laid to rest. In fact, far from warring against human responsibility for creation, Paul's view of human faith becomes, when rightly grasped, a key component in the whole scheme. How, then, does Paul see faith as the first and basic human response to God's act of faithfulness in Christ?

Abraham

Paul's major presentation of faith comes in Romans 4 and centers entirely around the person of Abraham. That Abraham rather than some other biblical figure should play this central role was dictated to a large degree by the Jewish tradition with which Paul was in dialogue in Romans. The prevailing view saw Abraham as principally a model of obedience: Abraham followed God's call to leave his country (Genesis 12), Abraham took on the command of circumcision (Genesis 17); above all, Abraham was prepared to sacrifice Isaac his son at God's command (Genesis 22). Against this view, Paul had to argue that Abraham was first and foremost a person of faith, that if he were obedient, which Paul did not deny, this obedience in a sense took second place. It *flowed from* — it did not *establish* — his relationship with God. First and basic to that relationship came faith.

A key aspect of Abraham's significance for Paul stemmed from the biblical tradition according to which the patriarch had received for himself "and his seed" the promise of "inheriting the Land" (cf. Gn 12:7, 15-17; 15:18; 17:8; 24:7; 26:4; 35:12). The "Land" originally referred to the actual land of Canaan, basically modern Palestine. But in the Jewish tradition which Paul presupposed the notion of the "Land" promised to Abraham had undergone a most notable extension. It was now seen as embracing the "whole earth." Thus Paul speaks of the "promise to Abraham and to his seed that he should *inherit the world*" (Rm 4:13). Moreover, along with this widening went the sense that God's promise to Abraham about the Land caught up the "inheritance of the earth" originally given to Adam in terms of the tradition in Genesis 1:26-28. The original bequest to Adam had in view the mastery of the present, created world. But when brought within the scope of the promise made to Abraham it acquired a future dimension as well. It was in fact seen to bear upon the destiny of human beings in the coming New Age. All the blessings of salvation, the whole "inheritance of the earth" intended by God for human beings from the start, were seen to be contained in the promise God made to Abraham "and to his seed."

For Paul, then, it was crucial to establish upon what basis Abraham received this all-important promise. Did Abraham earn his way into the receiving of this promise? Or did it come as pure gift from God, requiring only a living, grace-filled relationship established through faith?

Through a deft analysis of the exchange between God and Abraham told in Genesis 15, Paul shows (Rm 4:1-12) that Abraham received this promise on the basis of faith and not prior obedience. If we examine the exchange carefully we will note, as Paul obviously did, that in fact it contains two promises made to Abraham by God. The first promise was to the effect that Abraham and Sarah, advanced in years and childless up till then, would have a son and heir; ultimately their descendants would be as numerous as the stars of heaven (Gn 15:4-5). The promise concerning the Land — the one we have been considering up till now — followed upon this earlier promise concerning a son and heir. In between the two promises came a comment from the biblical writer crucial for Paul's purpose. The comment tells us that Abraham put his faith in the Lord and this "was reckoned to him as righteousness" (v. 6). That is, through his belief and trust that the Lord really would grant him a son Abraham was drawn into a "right" relationship with God. It was in the context of this right relationship established by faith that Abraham received, for himself and his descendants, the second promise, the "Land" promise, the one which contained in Paul's view, as we have seen, the "inheritance of the earth." It is from the sequence of these promises that Paul establishes the priority of faith in Abraham's relations with God.

Paul's chief intention in all this is not to discuss faith over against works in an abstract kind of way. As apostle of the Gentiles what he aims to prove above all is the truly broad scope of salvation, to show that in dealing with Abraham God had the whole world (the Gentiles) and not just the Jews in view. He plays upon the ambiguities latent in the Greek word for "nations" (*ethne*; the word was also used in the sense

"Gentiles") to show that Abraham's status as "Father of many nations" meant that the promise he received embraces the whole world and in fact actualizes the vision for the entire race spelled out in the creation accounts of Genesis 1-2.

In Paul's view this is the way it had to be since only so could God deal with human beings on the basis of grace — sheer undeserved gift — rather than merit (Rm 4:16-17a). It was impossible that God could be locked into a "works-reward," "employer-employee" relationship with human beings and still remain God. Employees who have done their work may demand their pay as a right. But such a schema operative in divine-human relations would give human beings a claim over against the Creator which would be simply untrue to the being of both. Abraham believed that God "graced" him just as he was, prior to any good work or achievement. This is the way it had to be because grace or gift was the sole basis upon which relationship with God could rest (Rm 4:4-5).

Here we touch the heart of Paul's theology of "faith alone." It stems from his central vision of God as Creator and human beings as creatures, whose basic response can only be gratitude, glory and praise. Paul pursues this vision of God in a deeper exploration of Abraham's original act of faith later in Romans 4 (vv. 17b-25). Abraham had to believe in God's promise that he would have a son in the context of his own advanced age and the barrenness up till then of Sarah his wife. Though it is not often apparent in the standard translations, on the side of both husband and wife Paul speaks of a "deadness" with regard to the faculties of procreation (v. 19). If Abraham was to have a child through Sarah, God would have to act as "One who brings the *dead* to life and calls into being things that do not exist" (v. 17) — in a word, act as Creator. Believing and hoping in God's promise of a son, Abraham believed in God precisely as Creator.

Significantly, in this connection, Paul adds the comment

(v. 20c) that in so believing Abraham "gave glory to God." To give glory to God is to acknowledge God as Creator in a way that reverses the pattern of the core of sin outlined in Romans 1:21-28. There, as we have seen, the process of sin is initiated when human beings worship the creature rather than the Creator, failing to "give glory and thanks to God as God" (v. 21). This failure to give glory to God results in their own loss of "glory" or likeness to God (v. 23), with all the dire results immediately spelled out as illustration of the "wrath." What Abraham does in his faith is precisely the opposite of this process. The "glory he gives to God in his believing, his trust and acknowledgment of the Creator, reverses the rebellion of sin, the "sin" story told "in Adam." It opens up for him and his descendants — believers of all generations — the "grace" story told in Christ.

Christian faith

Abraham is, of course, for Paul the paradigm of Christian faith. He sets the pattern that all believers follow. In a fine theological ending to the "treatise" on faith in Romans 4 (vv. 23-25) Paul brings all this home to Christian faith by pointing out that Christians also adopt the same pattern of faith. Like Abraham they too believe in a Creator God who brings the dead to life in the sense that they believe in "the One who raised Jesus our Lord from the dead, who was delivered up for our trespasses and raised for our justification" (vv. 24-25). They believe in God who was acting creatively in Christ to draw back the alienated world into right relationship with himself.

Faith, then, for Paul is that attitude which discerns God acting creatively in one's life and the world and which surrenders to that action in obedience and loving trust. It is through faith that human beings come under the scope of the promise "to inherit the world." In the story of Abraham, Paul shows how the original responsibility and gift, conferred upon Adam but forfeited when human beings follow the pattern of his sin, comes back through the right relationship with the Creator established by faith. Believers are the "seed of Abraham" to whom the promise is guaranteed.

Faith in this sense is in no way inimical to human responsibility for the world. On the contrary, faith is the very presupposition that the "grace story," rather than the "sin story" should prevail. From the human side faith is the only basis upon which right relationship with God can be established because it is the only basis which recognizes the true nature of both parties involved: God as Creator and human beings as creatures within a created world. The attempt to proceed upon any other basis is doomed from the start and, in Paul's view at least, turns rapidly into sin. As he remarks somewhat tartly later in the letter, "Whatever does not proceed from faith is sin" (Rm 14:23b).

Faith acknowledges that all I have, including my situation in the world and capacity to influence and develop it, is the gift of God. Faith also recognizes the human potentiality for sin and the ruinous consequences in terms of relationship both to God and to the world that flow therefrom. Faith reads the story of Jesus Christ, notably his death and resurrection, as God's gracious and ultimately victorious response to human sin and misbehavior in the world. It admits that true hope for the betterment of the world stems from human submission to and cooperation with the grace of God that comes in Christ. In a Pauline view all human activity, all human planning for the betterment of the world is off on the wrong foot if it does not somehow "connect" with grace.

Such a teaching on the primacy of grace and faith stands fair and square in the face of a purely secular humanism. It would contest the chances of making the world a better place without reference to some divine Being to whom all human beings are ultimately accountable. Believers, of course, must cooperate with those who do not share their faith in God. They will recognize in many instances greater generosity and dedication outside the bounds of explicit faith. But it will not be surprising if differences arise in plans, reactions and methods of approach. The Christian — and specifically Pauline — doctrine of the primacy of faith involves a distinctive view of the world and of human action within and for the world. It is in itself a true humanism — that is the whole point of Paul's view of Christ as the "Last *Adam*" rather than a stranger from some divine outer space. But it is a humanism which asserts that human beings can only be and remain truly human and humanize their world in so far as they live out and in some way acknowledge their all-important relationship with God.

In his attractive presentation of Abraham Paul paints a picture of a man who longed for a future — for himself, his family and his world — but saw an immense blockage: the sterility of his loins, which only the creative power of God could overcome. Abraham's life was drawn into an immensely fruitful project — the "inheritance of the earth" — because, as Paul shows, he surrendered himself in faith to God. He believed that God had the power and willing grace to carry out what was promised. It was following that commitment and within its scope that his obedience, his effect upon the world, flowed out in a fruitful way. In his believing Abraham sets the pattern for all who within a Christian commitment long to see and effect a better, more human world. It is now time to see how in Paul's view faith flows into Christian responsibility and love, how human beings are swept up into and cooperate with the faithfulness of God.

5.

CHRISTIAN OBEDIENCE

The last chapter attempted to show that there is no real opposition in Paul's view between faith and Christian action in the world. While this is so, the strong emphasis upon faith does present a problem. In working out a basis for Christian living Paul must walk something of a tightrope between two extremes. On the one hand, he has to retain his stress upon faith as that which alone initiates and preserves one's true relationship with God. But he must do so without downplaying the value of human activity, of what people do as distinct from what they might believe. To put it in more traditional terms: while allowing for genuine Christian responsibility in action, Paul must be careful not to re-erect a religion of "works" opposed to faith. He must avoid the possibility of human beings "going it alone" without reference to the Creator, allowing reentry to the subtle power of sin.

Characteristically, Paul solves this dilemma by focusing entirely upon Christ. One of his most distinctive ideas is that Christian life is life "in Christ." The phrase "in Christ" — or variants upon it — occurs over and over in the letters. Paul seems to envisage the Risen Lord as constituting a kind of corporate "sphere" of salvation "in" whom believers live out their lives. Sometimes he can turn the idea inside out, so that (the Risen) Christ himself lives "in" Christians. But normally it is the other way round. Christians live "in Christ" or "in the

Spirit" (the Spirit for Paul is virtually equivalent to the influence of the Risen Lord) in the same way as all human beings live in and breathe life from the atmosphere created by the air.

This idea of life "in Christ" has strong links with the "Adam" Christology which we have already studied at some length. Just as for Paul all human existence is somehow "contained" and typified by the career of Adam, so Paul sees that God has created fresh possibility for the human race by giving it a new founder whose vastly more positive and hopeful "story" believers can similarly share. Over against an unhappy solidarity in sinfulness and death "in Adam," there is the possibility of a community of life and hope "in" the "Last Adam," Jesus Christ.

What Paul has in mind in this view of Christian life is not a static enclosure in Christ but a dynamic insertion into what might be termed his total "career." By "career" I mean the full pattern of the life, death and resurrection of the Lord. Paul sums it up neatly when he speaks in Romans 8:17 of "sharing his sufferings, that we might also share his glory." But in Romans (6:3-10), we find a much more extended passage presenting this idea — one devoted precisely to the question of Christian behavior in the milieu of faith and grace:

> Do you not know that all of us who have been baptized into Christ Jesus were baptized into his death? We were buried therefore with him by baptism into death, so that as Christ was raised from the dead by the glory of the Father, we too might walk in newness of life. For if we have been united with him in a death like his, we shall certainly be united with him in a resurrection like his. We know that our old self was crucified with him so that the body of sin might be destroyed, and we might no longer be enslaved to sin. For he who has died is

> freed from sin. But if we have died with Christ, we believe that we shall also live with him. For we know that Christ being raised from the dead will never die again; death no longer has dominion over him. The death he died he died to sin, once for all, but the life he lives he lives to God. So you also must consider yourselves dead to sin and alive to God in Christ Jesus.

For Paul a reversion to life under the dominion of sin is (or ought to be) unthinkable for the Christian. This is because faith and baptism have effected a radical transfer from the "Adam" solidarity (the "body of sin" v. 6) to the new solidarity in Christ. The transfer is in fact so radical that Paul speaks of it in terms of a "death" to the old life. The baptismal union with Christ founds an entrance into his whole career — his death, burial and resurrection. The baptized have "died" with Christ. This means that they have done — or *should* have done — with sin once and for all. Paul, as we have seen, personifies sin and sees it as the rampant tyrannical power of the Old Age. Like all tyrants, it can have no claims upon one who has died. So "death," here, specifically the baptismal death in Christ, means release from the clutches of sin.

On the positive side, the baptismal union sets Christians in the direction of sharing the risen life of their Lord. I say "sets in the direction" because if we look closely at the passage from Romans 6 quoted above we will see that Paul carefully refrains from stating baldly that believers already share the full risen life of Christ. He says: "we *shall* certainly be united with him in a resurrection like his"; ". . . we *shall* also live with him." Full conformity to the risen life of Jesus is something yet to come, something that must await the resurrection of believers' own bodies.

But the resurrection does impinge on the present life of

Christians. Because of their existence "in Christ" the risen life of Jesus pulsates within them. It does this through the power of the Spirit, which well ups and shapes the pattern of Christian life. This is what Paul means by "walking in newness of life" (v. 4), by stating, "You also must consider yourselves dead to sin and living to God in Christ Jesus" (v. 11).

Living to God

Let us dwell for a moment on this idea of "living to God." For Paul "living to God" means allowing one's whole existence to be shaped by the fundamental openness and obedience to the Father that characterizes the total "career" of Jesus. Paul certainly thinks of Jesus as obedient in his earthly life — throughout the whole of life, but most notably in his passion and death, where Jesus became "obedient unto death, death upon a cross" (Ph 2:8). But there seems to be a sense in which Paul understands this openness to the Father as continuing also in his risen life. This explains the curious ending to the hymn quoted in Philippians 2: why it is "to the glory of God the Father" that "Jesus Christ is Lord" (Ph 2:9, 11); in 1 Corinthians 15 also we learn that the goal of Christ's messianic reign is that he "might hand over the kingdom to his God and Father" and be subject to him "that God might be all in all" (1 Cor 15:24-28). It is in this sense of continuing obedience and openness to the Father that Jesus "lives to God" (Rm 6:10b).

If Paul, then, is inviting Christians to think of themselves as dead to sin and "living to God in Christ Jesus" (Rm 6:11), he is really urging them to allow Christ to live out in them his continuing obedience to the Father. If the baptismal union with Christ means that Christians live "in" Christ and he "in" them, it also means that it is his obedience which must fundamentally shape their lives. Though still bodily anchored in the Old Age and in this sense still affected by the life "in Adam," believers are radically cut off from its control and are being "tugged" in the direction of the Lord's risen life. Their lives are being drawn into God's great project to usher in a New Age, the new possibility for human beings and their world that comes about in Christ.

Paul expresses this rather attractively when, towards the end of his exhortation, he urges Christians to "yield yourselves to God as people who have been brought back to life from the dead and your members as instruments of righteousness to God" (Rm 6:13). We have seen that Paul uses the idea of God's righteousness or faithfulness as the basic key to his understanding of what God is doing in Christ. As the eternally faithful One, God is reaching out in Christ to an errant, unfaithful world, to bring about the possibility of its fulfilling the original purpose of creation. God is overcoming the alienation, renewing the relationship and enabling the "grace" rather than the "sin" story to win out. By urging believers to offer their "members" — that is, their entire bodily existence — as "instruments of righteousness to God" Paul is picturing Christian existence as one where the whole moral life is placed at the disposal of this overarching project of God. It was this design that totally absorbed and explained the earthly existence of Christ. It continues in the obedience he renders to the Father through those who live "in him." The "good works" of Christians, therefore, are never their own achievement, something done over and against the grace of God. They are God's own creation, worked in believers, through the ongoing obedience of Christ.

In his letter to the Galatians Paul expresses the same idea in somewhat more personal terms. His basic task is to dissuade the Galatians from going back to the conditions of the Old Age by seeking to take on the yoke of the Jewish law. So he stresses the radicality of the break with the old existence that has come about for the Christian through faith and baptism:

> For I through the law died to the law, that I might live to God. I have been crucified with Christ; it is no longer I who live, but Christ who lives in me; and the life I now live in the flesh I live by faith in the Son of God, who loved me and gave himself for me (Gal 2:19-20).

Here we meet that same sense of "having died" to the past, of putting off an old "ego" and living a life totally swept up by Christ, where one "lives to God."

The cost of obedience

In a striking phrase Paul speaks of himself as having been "crucified with (literally 'con-crucified with') Christ." The tense of the Greek verb suggests that this "crucifixion," though initiated in baptism, is something which continues to place its stamp upon daily Christian life. The crucifixion of Jesus marked the high point of his earthly obedience — his "obedience *unto* death" (Ph 2:8). It was, as we have seen, the climax of a lifelong fdelity to the demands of being truly human in right relationship to God, one's fellow human beings and the world. The cross was the place where the cost of bearing that faithful witness in a world alienated from God came home with full rigor. So a Christian life, since it continues that same obedience, will involve a similar "crucifixion." The resurrection of Jesus may attest the dawning of the New Age. But the remnants of the Old still vigorously abound. Those who allow the faithfulness of God, the obedience of Jesus, to continue in their lives will find conformity to Christ a continual crucifixion.

This is how Paul accounts for his own apostolic trials and tribulations. "Always," he says (2 Cor 4:10-11), "we are carrying in the body the death of Jesus, always we are being given up to death for Jesus' sake." It is also the reason that, since earliest Christian days, baptism has been seen to find in martyrdom its perfect and culminating expression. The sense of obedience which lies at the heart of Paul's ethic for the New Age is ultimately a costly obedience because of the situation of the world. To live out fully one's baptismal bond with Christ, to "live to God" as he lived and lives to God, means surrendering one's life to the divine reaching out to reconcile, heal and humanize an alienated and frequently vicious world. This is the full measure of what Paul means when he urges the Romans to "yield your members as instruments of righteousness to God" (Rm 6:13).

Down the ages there has naturally been much preoccupation with the place of suffering in Christian ascetical life. Sometimes there has been the sense of suffering as something demanded by God as a test of love or a discipline to strengthen the soul. Devout Christians have embraced suffering voluntarily through fasting and other forms of penance. This tradition is venerable; it has been a feature of countless saintly lives. Paul, too, can speak at times in a rather ascetical way: "I drive my body and bring it into subjection, for fear that, after having preached to others, I may myself be disqualified" (1 Cor 9:27). My sense is, however, that his more characteristic tendency is not to see suffering as an individual ascetical exercise but rather as something flowing inevitably from deep personal union with Christ (Ph 3:10-11) and obedience to one's Christian calling in the world. As such it is not directly willed by God, any more than the suffering of Jesus was directly willed by God. It is the price of living in the world and for the world a life that is simply an outreach, an extension of the grace and love of God.

Conclusion: an ethic of responsibility

We have been considering Paul's understanding of Christian ethical life. I said at the start that he had to walk something of a tightrope in this area: allow for grace and faith in a way that did not undermine responsibility, but rather provided for that responsibility in a way that did not reintroduce a religion of "works." Paul's achieves this, I think, by seeing Christian behavior as flowing from faith and baptism and the union with Christ established thereby. As such it is an expression of the continuing obedience of Christ, the pure gift of God. It is not human achievement over against God, but the expression of God's grace drawing human activity freely and graciously into its scope.

Thus against an individualistic quest for perfection through good works, Paul sets an ethic of obedience flowing from faith. It might be called an "ethic of responsibility," since it sees Christian life as partaking in the responsibility of the Creator for creation. It is a truly humanist ethic because its whole aim is to be part of God's plan to bring the world to full humanity in Christ. All obligations, all rules flow from the question, "What does it mean to be responsibly human in this situation, in this world?" The measure is always the humanity of Jesus, crucified for his costly faithfulness, but raised as agent and exemplar of the humanity of the New Age.

The life of Jesus does not, of course, provide a model or answer to specific ethical dilemmas. The advance of technology, in particular, ever serves to increase the cultural distance between his historical situation and our own. In the face of every new issue we do not have scriptural blueprints, guidelines or rules. We have, rather, to ask, "What is the truly human, the truly responsible thing to do?" What the Pauline vision gives us is a sense of the total framework within which those questions must be asked — a sense of creaturehood and limit accompanying human dignity and worth, a sense of human responsibility for the world, a sense of the tug between human selfishness and God's grace, a sense that the truly human thing to do may also be the costly thing, at least in the here and now. For Paul it is not so much the life of Jesus that gives guidance in such things. It is what he calls the "mind of Christ," the disposition to continue his obedience, to allow his obedience to well up and find expression in each succeeding age. We still have to fill out the concept of Christian life for Paul. But this sense of responsible obedience is the foundation upon which all else is laid.

6.

CHRISTIAN FREEDOM

We have seen how Paul views Christian life as basically an existence swept up within God's faithful outreach to the world in Christ. Christian responsibility is, then, simply part of the overall responsibility of the Creator for creation — the living out of the vision sketched originally in Genesis 1. It is one thing, however, to know the basis of Christian ethics in Paul. It is another to be free to surrender one's life to this cause. Paul's concern in the central part of Romans is to show how it is both *necessary* and *possible* to live out the faithfulness of God, to be free to place oneself at the service of God's creative outreach to the world. It is time now to follow Paul some way into the mystery of Christian freedom.

The question of freedom is central for Paul because of his sense that the old "Adamic" existence is marked by a captivity to sin and death. When one becomes part of the New Age one "dies" to these tyrants and enters "in Christ" into a new realm of freedom. This freedom is double-edged: it is, at one and the same time, a freedom *from* the bind of these forces and a freedom *to* place one's life at God's disposal, to "live to God" as Christ lives to God.

In Romans 6, as we have seen, Paul indicates the objective basis of the liberation: the "entry into" Christ effected by baptism. Later on he explores the process of coming to freedom from a more psychological point of view. He sets the two situations, that of bondage and that of freedom in sequence (Rm 7:14-25 followed by 8:1-13) so that they can be compared — rather like two pictures making up a diptych. The combined effect makes for one of the most arresting and psychologically penetrating passages in his writing. Let us set out the texts side by side:

Rm 7:14-25	***Rm 8:1-11***
We know that the law is spiritual; but I am carnal, sold under sin. I do not understand my own actions. For I do not do what I want, but I do the very thing I hate. Now if I do what I do not want, I agree that the law is good. So then it is no longer I that do it, but sin which dwells within me. For I know that nothing good dwells within me, that is, in my flesh. I can will what is right, but I cannot do it. For I do not do the good I want, but the evil I do not want is what I do. Now if I do what I do not want, it is no longer I that do it, but sin which dwells within me. So I find it to be a law that when I want to do right, evil lies close at hand. For I delight in the law of God, in my inmost self, but I see in my	There is therefore now no condemnation for those who are in Christ Jesus. For the law of the Spirit of life in Christ Jesus has set me free from the law of sin and death. For God has done what the law, weakened by the flesh, could not do: sending his own Son in the likeness of sinful flesh and for sin, he condemned sin in the flesh, in order that the just requirement of the law might be fulfilled in us, who walk not according to the flesh but according to the Spirit. For those who live according to the flesh set their minds on the things of the flesh, but those who live according to the Spirit set their minds on the things of the Spirit. To set the mind on the flesh is death, but to set the mind on the Spirit is

members another law at war
with the law of my mind and
making me captive to the law
of sin which dwells in my
members. Wretched man that
I am! Who will deliver me
from this body of death?
Thanks be to God through
Jesus Christ our Lord! So
then, I of myself serve the law
of God with my mind, but
with my flesh I serve the
law of sin.

life and peace. For the mind
that is set on the flesh is
hostile to God; it does not sub-
mit to God's law, indeed it
cannot; and those who are in
the flesh cannot please God.
But you are not in the flesh, you
are in the Spirit, if in fact the
Spirit of God dwells in you.
Any one who does not have the
Spirit of Christ does not belong
to him. But if Christ is in you,
although your bodies are dead
because of sin, your spirits are
alive because of righteousness.
If the Spirit of him who raised
Jesus from the dead dwells in
you, he who raised Christ Jesus
from the dead will give life to
your mortal bodies also through
his Spirit which dwells in you.

Captivity

The passage on the left hand side (Rm 7:14-25) vividly describes the moral predicament of a person who desperately wants to do the right thing but finds within no capacity to carry out the good intention. Paul speaks in terms of the law of Moses because for him as a Jew it was this law that regulated all aspects of religious and moral life. Down the ages, however, readers and hearers of Paul have found that the experience he describes here resonates keenly with their own. Daily we find ourselves in the same dilemma: knowing what we should do, failing to summon up the strength, the energy, the self-discipline required to act. With Paul's contemporary, the Roman poet Ovid, we can exclaim: "I see the better way and I approve it. But I find myself following the worse."

So familiar in fact is the dilemma that we almost automatically assume that Paul is describing the darker days of ordinary Christian life. The fact that he speaks in the present tense throughout confirms the impression that it is Paul the Christian who speaks.

But matters are not so simple. If Paul speaks in the first person singular ("I") and the present tense, this could be simply a literary device designed to enhance the vividness of the description; it does not necessarily mean that he is describing his own experience past or present, or that he understands the moral conflict here described as something characteristic of present Christian life. One vital factor in present Christian existence is totally missing from this account: namely, the Spirit. The absence of the Spirit sets the passage in the starkest contrast to the one immediately following (8:1-4) where the Spirit rushes in as a liberating, life-giving force.

This suggests that the experience described in 7:14-25 is not "normal" Christian existence. To hold that Paul is referring to present Christian life is, admittedly, to be in good company in terms of the Christian tradition: Augustine (at least in his later writings), Thomas Aquinas, Luther, Calvin all saw the passage in this light and many still follow the same line today. But to retain this view is also to be set in the direction of a far more pessimistic spirituality than one truly grounded upon Paul's view of Christian life. What is described in 7:14-25 is the moral incapacity, the lack of freedom characteristic of life *prior* to or apart from the grace of Christ.

The real villain, of course, is the power of Sin, the rampant, infectious selfishness that fatally contaminates even the best desire on human part to do the right and good. Sin — personified here, as usually in Paul, as a tyrannical power — gets an ineradicable grip upon the "flesh." By "flesh" Paul does not mean the body or physical aspect of human nature — as though "sins of the flesh" in the traditional sense, especially sexual lapses, were *the* great manifestations of sin. Paul uses "flesh" in a scriptural sense, familiar from the Old Testament tradition, to denote simply human nature from the point of view of its being weak, fragile, mortal, set over against God, prone to rebellion and sin. A human life could be very pure in a bodily or sexual sense and still manifest "flesh" in terms of coldness, jealousy, self-seeking in other areas. "Flesh" is essentially human proneness to selfishness across all levels of existence — from the loftiest flights of intellect and spirit to the satisfaction of the most basic physical needs. It is in this sense that "flesh" provides for Paul a fertile field for Sin.

The struggle so graphically depicted in Romans 7:14-25 is the struggle of a person who keenly feels an obligation, who "delights in the law in the inmost self" (v. 22), but finds that the capacity or will to obey is simply not there. The obligation comes from outside, so to speak. It simply urges, insists upon what must be done. It does not lend any aid towards overcoming the resistance within. In fact, Paul's subtle analysis in terms of law shows that to confront human beings with moral demand in this external sense is to make matters worse by provoking a rebelliousness dormant hitherto. It is the "Adam" story all over again, replayed in every human life. To insist upon conformity to external moral norms, without addressing the basic inner problem — the proneness to self-doubt, uncertainty, rebellion within — is counter-productive in moral terms.

We hardly need Paul to persuade us that such is the case. The workings of the penal system in any society provide forceful evidence. Law and the penalties it imposes may restrain offenders for a time. More often, however, they serve only to exacerbate the deep-seated trauma within that leads people to anti-social behavior and offense — lack of self-esteem, anger, resentment against authority and so forth. Genuine, lasting rehabilitation will occur only when the inner problem is addressed, when human support and education lead to self-acceptance and inner healing. Then the values enshrined in the law — respect for others, for property, for the environment and so forth — values which the law could point to but not realize in the heart, these values can be internalized and take root within a person where they can be truly effective and influence behavior. Then, to use Jeremiah's image taken up by Paul, we can speak of a "law written in the heart" rather than on stone tablets (Jr 31:33; 2 Cor 3:3).

Freedom

Apart from such internalization of the law there is nothing but fatal tension and inability to act. This is the way Paul depicts the lack of freedom characteristic of the old "Adamic" age. When he has brought the description to its climax in v. 24: "Who will deliver me from the body of this death?," we hear at last the cry of discovery and release: "Thanks be to God, through Jesus Christ, our Lord" (v. 25a). The way then lies open to break through into the other panel of the diptych, to hear the account of freedom and release that has come about through what God has done in Christ:

> There is therefore now no condemnation for those who are in Christ Jesus. For the law of the Spirit of life in Christ Jesus has set me free from the law of sin and death For God has done what the law, weakened by the flesh, could not do: sending his own Son in

> the likeness of sinful flesh and for sin, he condemned sin in the flesh, in order that the just requirement of the law might be fulfilled in us, who walk not according to the flesh but according to the Spirit (8:1-4).

In stark contrast to the captivity, the incapacity and unfreedom described in 7:14-25, we hear in this passage a description of liberation, of capacity given — of a destiny to life rather than a servitude leading to death. Through what God has done in Christ, the Spirit has come into people's lives as a liberating, enlivening power. What the law required, but could not help to bring about, is now fulfilled in us through the indwelling Spirit.

We may note how insistent Paul is upon the *intimate* involvement of God's Son. In contrast to the law, which remains (ineffectually) "outside," Christ was actually sent "in the likeness of sinful flesh." Paul has no doubts about the personal sinlessness of Christ (cf. 2 Cor 5:21). But he is equally adamant that Jesus did not shrink from total involvement with the sinful human condition, what Paul calls the "flesh of sin." Dying between two thieves a death the Roman State reserved for slaves, rebels and the worst kind of social offenders, Jesus in every external way *looked like* a sinner. So intimate was his involvement that he was able to strike at the root problem — sin in the flesh — at its noxious core. Through Christ's act of total unselfish obedience and love, the truly effective remedy was applied. In the shape of the Spirit, the creative force of the New Age, a mighty source of unselfishness and freedom was unleashed in human lives.

We can perhaps grasp the force of the contrast Paul is setting up if we think of a social worker attempting to rescue a disadvantaged young person from constant conflict with the law. If a young teenager has had a family history of violence, parental conflict and neglect, it will not be surprising if encounters with the law serve only to increase inner tension, to provoke rather than deter temptations to offend. The values the law enshrines may be enlightened and good — something which the young person in more reasonable moments may be ready to accept. But they cannot be internalized in a lasting kind of way without some kind of healing within. This the social worker will try to promote by establishing a relationship on an individual basis, one that does not demand in the first instance a radical change in terms of behavior. Within the context of such a relationship, confidence, trust and self-acceptance can begin. And then may come the chance for an effective internalization of the values enshrined in the law. The process may be long, the cost to the social worker high in personal terms, but this is the only way in which the young person can grow towards responsibility and inner freedom.

In Pauline terms what the social worker has done is to "justify" the teenager while "ungodly," that is, establish a relationship *before* requiring change in behavior. This is what Paul sees God offering human beings through the work of Christ. Whereas the law could only make demands from without, Christ entered the human situation from within. Though he bore in his person the cost of overcoming the alienation, his obedient, faithful act released the Spirit of freedom and healing. This enables the values the law rightly required to well up from within and so effectively begin to shape behavior.

So it is that when human beings "enter into" Christ through faith and baptism, they enter into a sphere where the grace of the Spirit can become a liberating power in their lives, setting them free from the selfishness that is the mark of the grip of Sin. This and no merely external law is for Paul the only way in which it is possible to escape the subtle poison of sin, to place one's life effectively at the disposal of God.

In this connection we may note how, when speaking of the

new moral life in verse 4, Paul does not write, "so that we may fulfill the righteous requirement of the law," but "so that the righteous requirement of the law *might be fulfilled* in us. . . ." The passive construction is very deliberate. Paul wants to underline that the new moral capacity is in no way something we can exercise by ourselves. It is something worked in and through us by the Spirit. Any good we now perform is never our own achievement over against God. Were that the case, the aura of grace would fall away, we would not be in the sphere of the New Age but returning to the divisiveness from the Creator that marked the Old. The good works that now flow through the Spirit are the gift of God, the product of grace.[1] God does gather up human effort into his creative work; human activity does affect the future of the world. But ultimately all is cooperation with the power and faithfulness of the Creator, the fulfillment of the design laid out in Genesis 1 and 2.

If we glance back at these four verses taken as a whole what is striking is the totally Trinitarian character of Paul's view of Christian moral life. Into a human situation dominated by sin and alienation, *God (the Father)* sent the *Son (Jesus Christ)* to strike at the problem of sin at its deepest core. The unselfish act of Jesus, dying in love for sinners (while we were "God's enemies" Rm 5:10) released the *Spirit*, which became for all subsequent time the liberating force of the New Age. The Spirit is abroad for all time but its presence is tied for ever to what God has done in Jesus. It becomes effective in human lives in so far as believers allow the obedient pattern of Jesus' life to well up within them. In this way human lives become part of the ongoing creative work of God.

We are now perhaps in a better position to understand the full force of Paul's earlier injunction "to offer your members as instruments of righteousness to God" (6:13). "Righteousness," as we have seen, basically denotes the faithfulness of the Creator to creation. The crowning act of God's faithfulness was the sending of the Son to reconcile and give life to an alienated world. That faithful act of God continues in the Spirit, gathering up the lives of believers into its saving scope. Paul sums it all up aptly in another letter when he describes the goal of God's reconciling work: "God made him who knew no sin (that is, Jesus) into sin, so that we might become in him the righteousness of God" (2 Cor 5:21). It is not that we receive God's righteousness or simply acknowledge it. We actually "become" it in the sense that our lives are built into the ongoing faithfulness of the Creator to creation. It is for this high dignity that human lives have been set free.

The creative tension

Finally, in this matter of freedom, it is important not to neglect the warning that concludes the positive side of Paul's diptych (8:5-11). We are well aware of the tension building to a rending climax at the close of chapter 7. We sense the integration that comes with the breakthrough to chapter 8. What perhaps is not so obvious is the fact that even in the new life a certain tension remains. There are choices to be made. One can allow the pattern of one's living to be determined by the power of the Spirit and in this way be set on the path to life; or one can keep one's mind on the "flesh" and, in contrast, seek the ways leading to death. To put the matter in different Pauline language: you can follow the invitation of the Risen Lord to live with him the life of the New Age or you can choose to remain fixed in the Old. The one way leads to eternal life; the other ensures that physical death remains final.

The Christian has to live out daily this choice, has to live within this tension. The crucial difference between the tension described here and that in chapter 7 is that through the Spirit you do have a choice. It is certainly possible to "walk according to the flesh" and reap the fatal consequences. It is *possible*, but it is not *necessary*. You can opt for the Spirit and life; you do not *have* to live "according to the flesh," as was the case before. This is the crucial difference — the difference between enslavement and freedom.

Small wonder that this complete passage has exercised no little fascination for modern psychology. Across Romans 7 and 8 Paul provides a penetrating analysis of human behavior. Most psychologists would agree that a certain measure of tension — tension between goals and/or needs and the capacity to fulfill such aspiration — is necessary for human growth. Growth occurs when choices for life — sometimes hard, costly choices — are made rather than turned down or evaded; without such challenge human beings lapse into a form of existence little more than vegetative. There can come a point, however, when the gap between the goals or needs and the capacity to meet them can become too large, impossible of fulfillment. The tension becomes unbearable and ultimately destructive. It is no longer life-giving. It ends in enslavement.

My sense is that Paul's diptych illustrates both situations and describes the liberating transfer from one to another. In Romans 7 the tension is unbearable and ultimately destructive; in Romans 8 the Spirit creates the possibility of choices for life and freedom. If we mix up the two situations, seeing Romans 7 as addressing "normal" Christian life, we shall end up with a rather pessimistic, sin-weighted spirituality. If we keep Romans 7 for the pre-conversion situation and see Romans 8 as describing life in Christ, then we shall end up with a spirituality that is both realistic and hope-filled at the same time. It is realistic because it recognizes that in the present life, though under grace and the Spirit, we still have a conflict on our hands; the power of selfishness and sin must ever be resisted. It is hope-filled because it knows that the power of grace urging choices for life is stronger than the impulse to sin and death.

A test of spirits

Does this mean that the gripping account told in 7:14-25 must lose all relevance for Christian life? The fact that many Christians find in it something which resonates from time to time with their own spiritual lives should make us slow to agree. Within the tradition of spiritual discernment the passage can function as a sure "test of spirits." When we experience the conflict, the tension, the guilt — the despair even — which Paul describes, this can serve as a sign that we have lapsed back into a spiritual state of "pre-conversion" relationship with God. We feel trapped between a sense of our own weakness and the weight of moral obligations. The latter confront us simply as external law behind which there seems to stand the grim demand of a God who daily becomes less and less attractive. We feel we cannot gain divine acceptance unless we carry out this impossible obligation.

What has happened in fact is that we have turned away from Christ and the Spirit's power. We are trying to "go it alone" over against God. We forget that what God asks of us is, "in Christ," always gift and that Christ himself has joined us and remains with us in our weakness and even in our sin (8:3). What Paul has written can both help us recognize the predicament and point us back upon the right path. It invites us to turn away from fixation upon ourselves and our weakness to grasp again the grace of Christ welling up through the Spirit.

Concluding reflection

We have been considering Paul's account of the transfer from captivity to moral freedom made possible through the work of Christ. We have seen that the freedom of which Paul speaks is not a freedom from all restraint but a freedom to place oneself wholly and willingly at the disposal of the grace of God. This freedom does not exist in a vacuum but is part of the dignity and responsibility conferred by the Creator upon human beings according the vision of Genesis 1. If human beings relate to the world in the illusory freedom that is simply selfish exploitation in another guise, the effects upon the world will be patent; sin and not grace will have the upper hand. If human beings relate to the world with the true freedom that Christ confers, then the original design of the Creator will go forward. Creation continues in the work of grace. We must consider now how Paul relates this to the future in the second part of Romans 8.

FOOTNOTES

1. Though it does not cite this text of Paul, the Council of Trent in its Decree on Justification, Chapter 16, dealing with the question of merit, gives fine utterance to this same truth whereby the works of believers are entirely the creation of God without ceasing to be "our" works as well: "for that justice which is called ours, because we are justified by its inherence in us, that same is (the justice) of God because it is infused into us by God through the merits of Christ"; a few lines earlier the Decree speaks of the way in which Christ Jesus, with whom we are united as Vine and Branches (Jn 15:5), infuses strength into those justified, "which strength always precedes, accompanies and follows their good works" (DS 1546; translation from K. Rahner ed., *The Teaching of the Catholic Church* New York: Alba House, 1967, pp. 396-97. See also *The Christian Faith*, J. Neuner and J. Dupuis eds., New York: Alba House, 1982, pp. 563-564).

7.

HOPE FOR THE WORLD

We have mentioned from time to time the promise God made to Abraham and Paul's understanding of this promise as "the inheritance of the world" (Rm 4:13). I have argued that Paul's formulation of the promise in this way means that he sees its full working out as involving the human race's coming into that "possession" of the universe intended by God from the start but frustrated by human sin. This, in Paul's view, is the culmination of salvation, the completion of the work of Christ. In the chapters immediately preceding this one we have been looking at the human contribution to this process. We have been considering how Paul's sense of Christian obedience and Christian freedom imply human involvement in the creative work of God. We are now in a position to draw these various threads together and catch something of Paul's vision of the future as he sets it out in the latter half of Romans 8. Here, it seems to me, he most directly recaptures the vision of Genesis 1-3 because here he sets human hope in explicit relationship to the fate of the non-human created world.

Paul treats of human hope in the context of the one fact — suffering — that might seem to render it illusory. First of all in Romans 5 (vv. 1-11) and then, more extensively, in Romans 8 Paul tackles the problem of the continuing existence of suffering in what is supposed to be the dawning of the New Age. How can suffering continue to have a place in the new era of the

Risen Lord? If suffering is still around, is there any sense in which Christ's coming has changed the destiny of the world?

If the Old Age and the New were seen as destined simply to follow one another in a strictly defined sequence, then that charge would stand. But Paul's view of the "Ages" is, as we have seen, more complex than this. The resurrection of Jesus has, it is true, inaugurated the New Age. But the Old has not totally given way. Believers live in an era of "overlap" or "interpenetration" of the Ages. Two "stories" — that of the Old Adam and that of the New — run together in their lives. Though radically transferred through faith and baptism into the New Age, they are still bodily anchored in the Old. Total transfer to the New will come only with resurrection, when their bodies, too, take on full conformity to the risen body of the Lord (Ph 3:20-21).

In the meantime believers suffer in their bodies the onslaught and the temptations of the old era. They must live out the relationship with God appropriate for the risen life in the bodily conditions of the old. Though still "in the flesh" in the sense of present fragile human life, they have to live "not according to the flesh" but "according to the Spirit" (Rm 8:4, 12-13).

The new intimacy with God

The one element of the New Age that is most certainly complete is the relationship with God. Paul begins his outlook towards hope in Romans 8 by drawing attention to this.

> All whose lives are shaped by the Spirit of God are sons of God. For it is not a spirit of slavery that you have received — something to drive you back again to fear. But you have received a spirit of sonship, in

> which we cry out, "*Abba,* Father." The Spirit himself in this way bears witness to our spirit that we are God's children. And if we are children, then we are heirs as well — heirs of God, co-heirs with Christ (8:14-17a [author's translation]).

Alluding perhaps to an element in the early liturgy of baptism, Paul reminds his readers that the Spirit impels them to call upon God in the intimate form of address characteristic of Jesus. In his earthly life Jesus addressed God as "*Abba*" — something unknown in Jewish prayer up till that time. So distinctive was this address that the early Christian communities preserved it in Jesus' own language, Aramaic (cf. Mk 14:36; Gal 4:6), so as not to lose in Greek translation the particular nuance of the original. "Abba" was the way in which the Jewish child addressed the male parent within the intimacy of the family circle (though the usage could continue also into adult life). The address carried resonances of closeness, warmth, a sense of security and acceptance. It also looked trustingly to the future in the sense that it was from one's Abba that one could expect in due course to receive the family inheritance. This, presumably, is why Paul in the present passage forges a direct link between the "Abba" cry (v. 15) and the sense of being heirs — heirs of God, co-heirs with Christ (v. 17a).

Before turning to the future hope which this sense of inheritance implies, we may observe that in the "Abba" relationship with God there is restored — or gained for the first time — in the New Age the intimacy with the Creator that rings through Genesis 2. The Spirit banishes the fear and mistrust of God characteristic of the old, sin-dominated epoch. Welling up within believers is the sense of closeness and confidence that goes along with being made in God's image and entrusted with responsibility for the world. Adam sinned because in his heart there was sown a seed of mistrust, a doubt that the Creator would really be a God of grace, a God who would *give* the universe into human possession freely and without holding something back. In their "Abba" address to God believers expressly reject this doubt. The cry rings with the confidence that God as loving Father will most certainly confer the inheritance upon the human race.

One proviso is attached, in Paul's view, to this divine intent. Christians are heirs of God insofar as they are co-heirs with Christ. Their entrance into the inheritance must follow the pattern shown in him. Christ came into the inheritance as the one obedient unto death. In the hymn found in Philippians 2:6-11, the lordship of the universe (vv. 9-11) is conferred upon him precisely as the one who remained obedient unto death, even the death of the cross (v. 8). His suffering, as we have seen, was not exacted as a kind of price that had to be paid to God. Nor was it a test of worthiness for the inheritance. It was the cost that stemmed from embodying divine faithfulness and true humanity in the face of an alienated, sinful world. So when Paul writes, ". . . provided we are prepared to suffer with him in order that we might also share his glory" (Rm 8:17c), he is simply pointing out that those who share the obedience of Christ face a similar conflict with the remnants of the as yet unreconciled world. Christ continues his costly obedience in the bodily existence of believers. But it is through that obedience and through it alone that the world is brought into the New Age through the grace and power of God.

Creation groaning

Within this context of the mysterious link between suffering and the future hope Paul returns to set human beings explicitly in relationship to the non-human created world. We have seen a negative foreshadowing of this when early in Romans (1:18-32) he analyzes the core or nub of human sin. At heart it is all a matter of idolatry in that sin leads human beings to take the created world and misuse the gift of dominion. They either worship some aspect of it or exploit it in a way that becomes enslaving instead of mutually productive to the praise and glory of God. In the central part of Romans 8 (vv. 18-22) Paul takes up once again the theme of the interrelatedness of human beings and their world. Though he recalls the negative aspect of that relationship and does not lose sight of the suffering that marks the present age, the basic thrust is one of hope.

Let us set out the passage as it stands:

> [19]For creation waits with eager longing for the re-
> vealing of the sons of God. [20]For creation was sub-
> jected to futility, not by its own will but on account of
> the one who was meant to subdue it. And so the hope
> remained [21]that the creation itself would be set free
> from its bondage to decay so as to share the freedom
> associated with the glory of the children of God.
> [22]For we know that the entire creation has been
> groaning together in the pangs of childbirth right up
> till the present [author's translation].

Paul here personifies the non-human creation in a way that until recently, at least, would have sounded quite alien to modern ears. I say, "until recently" because Paul's view does now find some echo in *Gaia* and other present-day tendencies taking a personified view of the world.[1] For Paul, however, creation's whole intent is directed to the human race: it groans "with eager longing" awaiting the "revelation of God's sons."

The passage presupposes the Jewish tradition that saw the human and non-human creation locked in a "common fate" for good and ill. Non-human creation progresses when the human race progresses; it suffers a fall when human beings fall. The tradition goes back, of course, to the sense of responsibility for the world conferred in Genesis 1:26-28 and reiterated, after the Flood, in 9:7-17; it rests more precisely upon the story in Genesis 3:17-19 where the ground is cursed and becomes difficult to till because of Adam's sin. The same tradition, conversely, foresaw that restoration of human relations with God would be accompanied by a similar transformation of nature. So (Second) Isaiah, for example, spoke of the desert turning into a paradise for the exiles returning to Jerusalem (Is 41:17-20; 48:9-11; cf. Ezk 34:25-31; 47:1-2).

In the light of this tradition we can see why Paul can picture creation awaiting the "revelation of God's sons" with "eager longing." Since its own fate is so intimately bound up with that of human beings, it longs for them to arrive at the perfection which God intended for them from the start. That is, it longs for them to be revealed in their true dignity as "sons (children) of God." In line with the later Jewish tradition, Paul uses the image of divine sonship to designate those who have already entered or are destined to enter into full possession of the inheritance.

Within this overall framework Paul pictures creation longing for this to come about with a peculiar intensity and restlessness at the present time. The reason for the "restlessness" of creation is that it is presently condemned to futility" (v. 20a). By "futility" is meant frustration of its true purpose — as would be the case when a finely wrought violin has its back broken through some accident. At first glance it may still look intact, but it is fatally flawed, beyond repair. "Futility," then, is precisely the opposite of that "goodness" God saw in creation according to Genesis 1. Landscapes devastated by war, fertile areas reduced to desert by over-grazing, cities rendered uninhabitable by atmospheric pollution, irreplaceable forests cut down: all these modern symptoms of human misuse of creation would precisely correspond to "futility" in Paul's understanding.

Alluding to the "Fall" story of Genesis 3, Paul explains that creation is "restless" because this lapse into futility was not something of its own doing or something that it wanted at all. Rather it was dragged down, willy-nilly "because of the one who was meant to subdue it" (v. 20b).

Who is this "subduer"? Most current translations of the text imply that the "subduer" is Gòd. However, there are good grounds for holding that by the "subduer" Paul means the one who, according to the original design sketched out in Genesis 1-3, was meant to "subdue" the earth, namely, the entire human race in the person of Adam. In other words, we have here an allusion to the vision of the creation accounts according to which the world finds its proper fulfillment only in relation to human beings — and vice versa. Having fallen because the human race has chosen to frustrate its own relationship to God and never accepting that state of affairs as final, creation cherishes a hope that it too will benefit when relations between God and human beings are set right in Christ.

The implication is that, as the rest of the created world has suffered and suffers when the "Adam/sin" story runs, so it benefits, is liberated from "futility" and brought to its proper purpose when the "Christ/grace" story runs. Paul points to the groaning of creation in support of his case for hope, the hope that the latter rather than the former "story" will win out in the end. Creation groans in the pangs of childbirth; it "suffers together" up till now (v. 22). But birth pangs are sufferings redolent with hope. Hope for the future springs from the fact that the "weighting," the greater force, rests with grace, rather than with sin (Rm 5:15-21).

Paul's view of creation personified and "groaning" stems

from Jewish apocalyptic imagery current in his time. We can hardly take it seriously, at least in any literal sense. Probably he was himself conscious of sketching a powerful imaginative vision rather than arguing in strict sober logic. Nonetheless, I would maintain that in this curious passage he invites us to see the original vision of Genesis coming true in Christ. The human responsibility for creation outlined in Genesis 1-3 redounds for good and ill upon the future of the world. When, following the disobedience of Adam, human beings allow the "sin" story to run, that story leaves its destructive smudge upon the world, its devastation increasing as technology ensures its ever more widespread application. When, on the contrary, the obedience of Christ prevails, then God's original design goes its life-enhancing way.

Responsibility and hope

The upshot is, surely, that the future of the world is very much in human hands — where God left it or leaves it according to Genesis 1 and 9. This does not mean that God sits back and does nothing. On the contrary, God is ever active as Creator. But human beings play a central role in God's creation of the future of the world precisely as they allow themselves to be "in Christ" the instruments of grace, "yield their members as instruments of righteousness to God" (Rm 6:13). Then human life, human activity is "built into" the work of creation. As Paul so strikingly puts it (2 Cor 5:21), we "become" in Christ "the righteousness of God," the faithful responsibility of the Creator for the world.

In this perspective the world is not some kind of vast playpen in which God lets us act out our lives for a time, testing us to see if we are suitable to live in some other realm. Undoubtedly there are strands in our biblical tradition, including some of Paul's letters, that give rise to such a view. However, in his mature exposition of the gospel in Romans, Paul does seem to posit a genuine continuity between this present world, sin-stained and death-laden though it is, and the life of the world to come. It is true he speaks of "resurrection," of the "redemption" of our mortal bodies from their attachment to this passing world (8:23). And resurrection seems to imply a moment of radical discontinuity, of passage from the present form of life to one of a totally new dimension (1 Cor 15:35-57; 2 Cor 5:1-5). In Romans, however, one has the sense that Paul understands resurrection more in terms of transformation, rather than of destruction and beginning all over again.[2]

This transformation Paul sees also as the goal of our own longing: "And we too, having the first fruits (of salvation) in the shape of the Spirit, groan as we await full sonship, the redemption of our bodies" (Rm 8:23-25). The Spirit engenders within Christians a restlessness with their present lot. The restlessness does not imply longing to be taken out of the present created world but a longing that its present death-determined structures be transformed. The Spirit gives the sense that what we have now is neither what should be nor what will be if the design of God wins through. What ultimately the final shape will be we cannot now see; as Paul says (v. 24), a hope already in view is not really a hope at all (v. 24). Prompted and encouraged by the Spirit we pray for and labor towards a future wrapped in the still unfolding plan of God (vv. 25-28).

Though unable — and unconcerned (contrast 1 Th 4:13-18) — to give any detailed sketch of the future, Paul makes clear one central and essential truth: the ultimate goal of God's design is that we should become "sharers in the image of his Son" (v. 29). By this Paul understands that we should take on the "image of God" way of being that is proper to Christ as "Last Adam" and Risen Lord (see 2 Cor 4:4 where Paul speaks very attractively of "the light of the gospel of the glory of Christ, who is the image of God"). When human beings are conformed to the Risen Lord in this way, then God's original design for creation will be achieved. Human beings will have reached their full dignity together and in harmony with the created world in which they have been placed.

In this view, as already noted, human "works" really do contribute to the future of the world — an aspect of Paul's thought particularly congenial to the Catholic tradition. God creates the future of the world, but draws human beings into the process all the while. This human cooperation is, of course, something which can work in two directions: one good, one ill. The apocalyptic perspective of the "end of the world," so often seen as something God would do, really lies in human hands. Our way of life, our technology can destroy the world: through environmental devastation, nuclear exchange, genetic manipulation, even, as we have been so sharply reminded recently, financial irresponsibility. Such a fate would be the result of letting the "sin" story prevail.

Respecting human freedom, the Creator takes this risk, places the fate of the earth in human hands. At the same time in the redemptive work of Christ the Creator addresses the ravages of human sin, faithfully reasserting the more powerful claims of grace. Entrenched, established as they are, the patterns of sin ensure that obedience to grace carries its cost — as it did supremely in the case of Christ. For this reason it is in the context of suffering that Paul points to the emergence of hope. But, no stranger himself to suffering and weakness of the flesh (see esp. 2 Cor 11:23-28; 12:7-10), he nonetheless proclaims most boldly the ultimate triumph of grace. "If God is for us, who is against us?" (v. 31). If God "did not spare his own Son, but gave him up for us all, how could he fail to give us along with him all things?" (v. 32). "All things" presumably refers to that "inheritance of the earth," promised to Abraham, now in Christ being brought to realization.

Conclusion

What emerges ultimately from all this is a vision of the future of the world that attempts to hold both the divine and the human contribution together. Hope for the future does not derive simply from an optimistic view of the present situation. It does not mean that if human beings ruin the world, the Creator will affect a kind of final *deus ex machina* rescue. Nor, in contrast to a Marxist view, does hope spring from the necessary working out of socio-economic forces in a deterministic kind of way. It springs ultimately from the fidelity of the Creator to creation and from a sense that fidelity can, through grace, prevail in the human sphere.

It is in this sense, it seems to me, that we must read Paul's concluding exhortation:

> I am persuaded that neither death nor life, neither angels nor principalities, neither things present nor things to come, neither powers nor height or depth nor any created thing, will be able to separate us from the love of God that comes to us in Christ Jesus our Lord (vv. 38-39; author's translation).

We can identify the forces of death and life in our own situation. We can nominate the "principalities and powers," and bring "down to earth," so to speak, concepts that in Paul's language sound other-worldly and remote. To my mind, they were not for Paul other-worldly at all; they were very real "worldly" forces with which he had daily to contend and which he catalogues at length in several places (2 Cor 4:8-12; 6:4-10;

11:23-27). Paul is convinced that as instruments of sin they will not prevail because as resurrection witness he knows they did not prevail against the obedience of Christ. In his vision of the Risen Lord, he has glimpsed both the New Adam and the New Age. In his conviction of God's love and his lived experience of the Spirit he is confident that he can proclaim the dawning of that New Age even in the present, suffering world.

FOOTNOTES

1. See J.E. Lovelock, *Gaia: A New Look at Life on Earth* (Oxford and New York: Oxford University Press, 1979; N. Myers (ed.), *Gaia: An Atlas of Planet Management* (New York: Anchor, 1984).
2. We can see the same tension between a more "discontinuous" view of the future world and one which emphasizes transformation of present structures in the Vatican II Pastoral Constitution *The Church in the Modern World (Gaudium et Spes)*, especially 39: "We do not know the time for the consummation of the earth and of humanity. Nor do we know how all things will be transformed. As deformed by sin, the shape of this world will pass away. But we are taught that God is preparing a new dwelling place and a new earth where justice will abide; later, the expectation of a new earth must not weaken but rather stimulate our concern for cultivating this one. For here grows the body of a new human family, a body which even now is able to give some kind of foreshadowing of the new age. For after we have obeyed the Lord, and in His Spirit nurtured on earth the values of human dignity, brotherhood and freedom, and indeed all the good fruits of our nature and enterprise, we will find them again, but freed of stain, burnished and transfigured" (W.M. Abbott ed., *The Documents of Vatican II* London: Chapman, 1967 p. 237). The same stress upon the value of "this-worldly" activity can be seen taken even further in the Statement "Justice in the World" issued by the Second Synod of Bishops, 1971, which insisted, "Action on behalf of justice and participation in the transformation of the world fully appear to us as a constitutive dimension of the preaching of the Gospel" (6) (Text given in J. Gremillion, *The Gospel of Peace and Justice* New York: Orbis, 1976 pp. 513-29).

8.

LIFE IN THE BODY

There is no idea that Paul exploited more richly for his purpose than that of "body." By "body" (Greek *soma*) Paul understood the physical body — the material side of human make-up. But "body" had for him also a further connotation not always present in our use of the term today. "Body" for Paul meant principally the medium of communication between an individual and the outside world of persons and events. It is through my body that I give and receive impressions. It is through my body that I stand in relationship to others, that I am "in touch" with them and they with me. *Bodily* I belong to the surrounding world, bodily it impinges upon me. So fruitful was this idea for Paul that he placed it at the center of his understanding of Christian life, especially as regards the social dimension. Our understanding of Paul's spirituality of the world would be incomplete were we to neglect this aspect of his thought.

Discussing Paul's view of the "Two Ages," the Old and the New, and the way they interpenetrate at the present time, I said that Christians have the task of living out the relationship to God appropriate for the New while *bodily* anchored in the Old. It is in the "body" that they feel — often painfully — the opposing pull of both allegiances. The present mortal body is the means of belonging to the Old Age. Destined to death, it suffers the continuing onslaught of the forces of sin and death.

But the dawning of the New Age holds out the prospect of resurrection, of a bodily existence patterned after that of the Risen Lord. In a phrase that can sound contradictory if not rightly understood, Paul speaks of the new existence as involving a "spiritual body" (*soma pneumatikon*: 1 Cor 15:44). By this he does not mean a way of being that is in some sense "immaterial" but rather a bodily life that is vivified by the Spirit.

This destiny to a future existence that will be in some sense bodily makes for the dignity and value of the *present* life in the body. Paul uses this argument to take to task a party within the Corinthian community who devalue present bodily existence on the grounds that they have entered the New Age once and for all and can leave that sort of thing behind. The insignificance attributed to the body can lead, on the one hand, to an abandonment of all restraint in sexual relations (see Paul's warning against fornication in 1 Cor 6:12-20); on the other hand it can induce some to forbid marriage or sexual relationships altogether (1 Cor 7). In particular, it can lead to the devaluing of simple service rendered to one's neighbor because of a sense that one is caught up and away in a religious realm removed from such mundane concerns (1 Cor 8). The Corinthians falsely interpret the present gift of the Spirit as an indication that they are living totally in the New Age and can ignore the claims of the here and now. Against such "other-worldly" tendencies Paul has to insist that the Christian task is precisely to live out the life of the Spirit in the present bodily situation. This means relating to the present world, passing though it may be, and taking its claims seriously.

It is, as we have seen, "in the body" that such claims are met. Christian obedience is bodily obedience — standing bodily in the world, as Christ stood faithfully in the world. The human relationship to the rest of creation described in Genesis 1:26-28 is relationship through the body. That is why human existence remains bodily existence in the New Age as well as in the Old. Even if Paul can occasionally describe the Christian as having a "citizenship" that is "heavenly" (Ph 3:20), he goes on in the very next sentence to describe that existence as consisting precisely in the conforming of our (present) lowly bodies to the pattern of the glorious *body* of Christ: "But our citizenship is in heaven, and from it we await a Savior, the Lord Jesus Christ, who will change our lowly body to be like his glorious body, by the power which enables him even to subject all things to himself" (v. 21).

Paul can sometimes speak in a disturbingly negative way about the body. Thus in Romans 8:13 he warns, "If you live according to the flesh you will die, but if by the Spirit you put to death the deeds of the body you will live." It would have been more consistent to have written, "put to death the deeds of the *flesh*." In any case the context shows that "body" is to be understood here as more or less equivalent to "flesh." Paul is thinking of bodily action that is totally determined by the conditions of the present, passing age. When through the power of the Spirit one "puts to death" the selfish impulse of the "flesh," bodily action is transformed into something which belongs to the dawning of the New Age. The difference is that whereas "flesh" is always negative or at least neutral (in the sense of merely physical), "body" can go in two directions: towards the Old Age or towards the New. Thus Paul can speak of the "resurrection" (or "redemption": Rm 8:23) of the body, where he never speaks of the "resurrection of the flesh."

There is no doubt, then, that in Paul's view human beings can and indeed have to relate to God and the New Age in terms of "body." Put the other way round, the interrelatedness to the rest of the creation which comes about through the body is part of the belonging to the New Age as it was to the Old. And the transformation which this implies, though outwardly complete only in resurrection, is already under way. It comes about as

Christians "put to death" in the Spirit the claims of "fleshly" bodily existence (Rm 8:13b) and instead "offer their members as instruments of righteousness to God" (Rm 6:13).

Community life in the body

So far we have been speaking of Paul's view of individual Christian existence "in the body." More distinctive, however, is his sense of communal existence as "life in the body." Up to a point Paul's use of "body" with respect to Christian community life is purely metaphorical. He employs the image of the human body to describe the various functions and gifts within the community and the way they should operate in mutual harmony for the common good (see especially 1 Corinthians 12). In so doing he is only making use of a stock metaphor to be found in many writers of his time, notably the Stoics, who used the "body" image to emphasize the unity of the human race.

Paul has a tendency, however, to bring this image into his vision of how believers relate to the Risen Lord. We have already noted the way in which Paul pictures Christian existence as life "in Christ," that is, a living "in" the Risen Lord as in a corporate "sphere of salvation." It is a short step from this idea to that of Christians making up Christ's "body," so that the simple metaphor takes on a Christological reality. The transition is easy if we remember the basic connotation of "body" as medium of union and communication. Believers make up the "body of Christ" in virtue of their intimate union with the Risen Lord on the one hand and with their fellow Christians on the other. So Paul writes:

> For just as the body is one and has many members, and all the members of the body, though many, are one body, *so it is with the Christ.*

> For by one Spirit we were all baptized into one body
> — Jews or Greeks, slaves or free —
> and all were made to drink of the one Spirit (1 Cor 12:12-13).

The observation, "so it is with the Christ," suggests that at this point (v. 12) we have moved from mere metaphor to a sense of the entire community (which is for Paul first and foremost the local community rather than the world-wide Church) making up one Person, "the Christ." All relationships between believers are underpinned by the fundamental relationship to the Risen Lord whose "body" they communally comprise.

Earlier in the same letter (1 Cor 10:16-17) Paul had expressed a similar idea in relationship with the communion established both with the Lord and with each other through participation in the Eucharist:

> The cup of blessing which we bless, is it not a communion in the blood of Christ? The bread which we break, is it not a communion in the body of Christ? Because there is one bread, we, many though we are, are one body, for we all partake of the one bread [author's translation].

By "communion in the body of Christ" Paul is not thinking exclusively of sharing in the body of Christ in the form of the eucharistic bread. He has in mind — perhaps uppermost in mind — the communal union with the Risen Lord constituted by and celebrated in the eucharistic participation.

As we noted above, Paul turns to the "body" image most notably when dealing with the issue of "spiritual gifts" within the community. The Pauline communities recognized the Spirit poured out upon them and moving in their midst as not just a generalized kind of gift but one which showed itself in different ways in different individuals. Each one had his or her own distinctive share of the Spirit in the shape of a particular gift, for which Paul uses the attractive Greek word *charisma*. The Corinthians appear to have prized one particular gift of the Spirit — speaking in tongues — above all others; they tended to regard tongues as *the* gift *par excellence*, despising the rest. What Paul does in 1 Corinthians 12 is to insist upon both the variety of gifts and the way in which in their variety they all together build up the life of the "body." Alongside "tongues," which he puts rather low down upon the scale, he also lists gifts of faith, of healing powers, insight, discernment, leadership, administration and humble service (vv. 28-31). And he points (Chapter 13) to the supreme gift — love — without which all the others are empty.

Because the gifts stem from the Spirit, they manifest the "new creation." In fact, we might well go so far as to define "spiritual gift" (*charisma*) in Paul as the distinctive share each one is given in the power of the new creation (the Spirit). Paul, as we have noted, understands the Risen Lord to be the One who first and foremost successfully plays out the role, originally sketched for Adam, of "subduing" the universe to the glory of God. In this connection, later in the letter (1 Cor 15:25-27a), he quotes Psalm 8 with respect to the messianic reign of Christ:

> For he must reign until he has put all his enemies under his feet. The last enemy to be destroyed is death. *For he (God) has put all things in subjection under his feet* (Ps 8:6).

The "reign" Christ exercises here is not a passive status. It is an active "subduing" of the universe to the glory of God. It is true that Paul interprets Psalm 8 "messianically." That is, he takes it to be referring in the first instance to Christ's messianic rule rather than to the role and status of human beings in general. But this Christological interpretation in no way overthrows the original meaning. Through the gifts bestowed by the Spirit believers have a share in Christ's messianic reign. "In Christ" they help bring to fulfilllment the wider vision of the psalm. The separate gifts of the one Spirit make the believing community a microcosm — a beachhead, one might say — of the new creation.

The prophet's gift

Writing to the Corinthians Paul is particularly at pains to sort out the relationship between two gifts: "tongues" and "prophecy." In the face of the community's clear preference for the more dramatic manifestations of the Spirit, Paul wants to commend the prophet's gift. "Prophecy" in the early Church did not necessarily connote, as in modern understanding, an ability to tell the future. It meant, rather, the gift of discerning what the Spirit was saying to the "body," the Church, in this particular concrete situation.

Put in more strictly Pauline terms, it was the prophet who had the gift of discerning the claims of the new creation in the context of the old.[1] We have noted the idea of the "overlap" of the Ages in Paul's understanding of Christian life — how Christians are called to live the life of the New Age in the bodily conditions of the Old. In this situation there is a constant temptation to settle back into the Old, especially in the area of social obligations — to let the old distinctions "Jew and Greek, slave and free, male and female" (Gal 3:27) prevailing in the surrounding unbelieving world, set the pattern within the community as well. It is the prophet's task to insist upon the pattern dictated by the Spirit of Christ rather than the spirit of the world. The prophet feels the "tug" of the New Age with peculiar sensitivity.

The prophet, then, speaks in the name of the Risen Lord, anointed with the Spirit. She or he indicates where the structures of society or Church do not reflect the values of the New Age into which the community is being drawn. So it may be that structures such as slavery, the subservience of women, the stockpiling of weapons of mass destruction can be accepted for a time in the community. Eventually prophets arise to point out — often abrasively, offensively — that such situations do not reflect the gospel of Christ, cannot be part of the new world that in the Spirit is struggling to be born, do not reflect the faithfulness and responsibility within the universe required of human beings by God.

Of all the gifts of the Spirit described by Paul prophecy is the one that the Church has found hardest to live with. It is, in fact, probably true to say that prophecy in the New Testament sense ceased to be recognized as a gift after the early centuries. But perhaps it is prophecy, more than any of the other gifts, that the Church is being called upon to recognize, own and test at the present time.

The eucharistic body

It is in the context of the Eucharist that Paul's sense of the Church as "body" reaches the finest point of focus. His critique of the way the Corinthians celebrate the Eucharist (1 Cor 11:17-34) does not concern what might be called the more "ritual" aspect of the sacrament. What worries Paul is the surrounding social context. The early Christians celebrated the Eucharist within the framework of a meal taken together. At Corinth the conduct of this meal served only to highlight social divisions. Through an unequal sharing of food or through consuming all there was before everyone was present the more affluent members of the community deprived those too poor to bring anything with them. This, in Paul's view, was to "despise the Church of God" (v. 22b).

To make his point in the face of such behavior Paul recalls the Eucharistic tradition — what he "received from the Lord and handed on to them" (vv. 23-25). The blessed and broken bread is the "body" given up for the brethren. The rite proclaims the death of the Lord as an act of selfless love. To celebrate it in a context where those present are not caught up in the rhythm of that same love, where in fact that love is injured, is to distort the sacrament's whole meaning. It is to eat and drink judgment to oneself, rather than healing and salvation (vv. 27-34).

Paul describes such a false celebration as "not discerning the body" (v. 29). This curious phrase has traditionally been taken to indicate failure to discern in the sacrament the "real presence" of the Lord. But the question of "real presence" was an issue for the later Church rather than for Paul. The Corinthian abuse in Paul's eyes is not failure to discern the Lord's presence but the way in which the *mode* of that presence should bear upon the situation of the poorer members. The Corinthians are "not discerning the body" in the sense that they are failing to see that they are gathered as the "body of Christ," that is, as the living "extension" of his person in space and time. What they proclaim in the eucharistic words and what they enact bodily in their community cannot be at odds. It is all the one "Christ" that is involved.

There is, then, a firm continuity between Paul's sense of the community as "body of Christ" and the eucharistic "body." To celebrate the Eucharist is to celebrate bodily union with the Lord. The rite overflows into the social context and makes demands upon it. It summons all those who partake of the broken bread to be caught up in the rhythm of the Lord — his self-giving love, his faithful obedience in the body. The Eucharist for Paul is not a private rite of comfort for the initiated, cut off from the world. It is ordained to the celebration of that "life in the body" in all senses to which believers are, in Christ, summoned. It impels towards responsibility — first to the community, then to the wider world in which believers, like Christ, live out their bodily obedience. It is an anticipation and a pledge of the universal "communion" (*koinônia*) that is to mark the full arrival of the New Age.

"Body of Christ" in later Pauline literature

I have suggested that, when the implications are fully teased out, Paul's sense of the Eucharist and the Church as "body of Christ" has reference not just to the community but to the wider world. To some extent this wider "extension" of his thought is found already in the new Testament itself. The later letters, Colossians and Ephesians, written within a Pauline school rather than by the apostle himself, develop the "body of Christ" idea in this direction. Here it is the entire world-wide Church, not just the local community, that makes up the "body of Christ." And as "body," in the Pauline sense, the Church forms the medium of communication between the Risen Lord and the surrounding world: it is the "fullness" (Greek *plêrôma*) of the one (Christ) who fills all things in all (Ep 1:23). Christ as "head" deals with the world through his "body" which is the Church. The Church, made up of two communities (Jews and Gentiles), once at enmity, now reconciled in Christ, functions as sacrament of God's power to effect a more universal reconciliation (Col 1:15-20; Ep 1:22-23).

As I said, Paul himself does not go this far. But the development is a faithful extension of his idea of Christian life as life "in the body of Christ." It has particular relevance for the spirituality we are attempting to draw out from his writings with respect to Christian relating to the world. It suggests that not only individual Christians, but the Church as a whole and individual churches (in the [more strictly Pauline] "local" sense), have a role in both embodying and facilitating — not without cost — the coming of the New Age in the world.

Conclusion

A spirituality that is genuinely based upon Paul must recognize both the range and subtlety of his use of "body." Interpretation in this area can be most fruitful; here it can also go disastrously wrong. The important thing is to grasp the way in which "body" functions within Paul's sense of Christian life as a living within the "overlap" of the Ages.

The temptation has always been to move towards one extreme or the other, seeking escape from the ambiguity of the present time. Like the Corinthians, believers can seek to ignore the body and live in the Spirit as if the New Age had wholly arrived; this will lead to both social neglect and a perfectionism impossible to fulfill. On the other hand, forgetful of the freedom already won by Christ and sensed in the Spirit, believers can be tempted to return to the fear and crushing legalism of the past. This is to emulate the Galatians who sought to place upon their bodies — in circumcision — the mark of the old era.

In response Paul had to try to restore the balance: to bring both back to the center away from the false simplicity of the extremes. His task, as teacher and pastor, was to fight for the recognition that present Christian life is life "in the overlap," where both Spirit and "flesh" make their claim upon the body and call for a daily discernment. As long as attitude towards the body remains a preoccupation and a test for believers, we will find in Paul much to instruct and challenge us.

FOOTNOTES

1. I have developed this understanding of "prophecy" more fully in an article, "Prophecy Now: the Tug into the Future," *Way* 27/2 (April 1987) 106-116.

POSTSCRIPT

We have been seeking to find in Paul a basis for a Christian spirituality of the world — a spirituality, that is, that takes seriously not only the relationship with the divine but the relationship to the total environment of the human as well. I have suggested that if we look closely at the extent to which the creation traditions function in Paul's writing, an apt basis for such a spirituality can be found in his thought. Paul understood that what God was doing in Christ was bringing the original design of creation to its full fruition — exercising fidelity as Creator in the face of the frustration of creation by human sin. Paul also understood that central to that plan was the foundation in Christ of a new humanity in which a "grace" rather than a "sin" story might run — with effects that redound not only upon human beings but also upon the world for which before God they are responsible.

Paul may come across in the New Testament as the most breathlessly active of apostles. But the attitude that would seem to underpin his theology is one that is at base *contemplative.* Paul's stance is truly contemplative because it is one which seeks to restore and respect the autonomy of all: to let God be God, to let creatures — human beings and the rest of creation — be creature. This to my mind is the attitude that should truly emanate from the Old Testament creation tradition, including that aspect of it which assigns a wider responsibility to human beings. The contemplative attitude is set over against the *exploitative* attitude which places "I" at the center and subjects all else to my needs, projects and insecurities. As we noted early on, this unwarranted exaltation of "I" is for Paul the heart of sin. It despoils creation and brings ever closer the threat of global devastation.

The contemplative attitude is exercised in prayer because it is in prayer that I learn to sit for a time simply with my creaturehood, trying to find and rest content with my proper place in the scheme of things. Prayer that is truly contemplative requires removal from preoccupation with "I" in simple respect for the being and the beauty of all else. Prayer invites me to let go of the "I" that seeks to control, to order, to be in charge. It is in prayer that I begin to experience that "death" of the Ego of which Paul spoke when he wrote to the Galatians about the new order which one enters in Christ: "I have been crucified with Christ; it is no longer I that live, but Christ who lives in me" (2:20a). I am compelled to be silent, to listen — to wait upon the messages that come not only from God but from the rest of creation as well.

It is interesting that just after speaking of creation's restless "groaning," Paul addresses the question of Christian difficulty in prayer: "When we do not know what to pray for," that is, when our hope wavers because we cannot see or even imagine the future God has in store, "the Spirit comes to our aid with sighs too deep for words" (Rm 8:26). Within our being, at a level too deep for ordinary consciousness to plumb, Paul is certain that we are caught up in a divine exchange of love. At this depth, accessible only to faith, the barrier between present reality and future hope begins to fall away.

There is, then, no tension at all — in Pauline terms — between a truly contemplative attitude and commitment to an active exercise of Christian responsibility for the world. To acknowledge that the future of the world lies in human as well as divine hands and to seek to take that responsibility seriously flows essentially from contemplation and a sense of the transcendence of God. It is only when the "grace" or "gift" aspect is ignored, when action ceases to be obedience that the way to exploitation lies open.

Ultimately the cost of obedience and the cost of contemplation are one. Both involve turning away from the demands of "I," the losing of one's life in order to save it (Mt 10:39; Mk 8:35; Lk 17:33; Jn 12:25), following the pattern of Christ who "did not please himself" (Rm 15:3).

The resurrection of Jesus, the selflessly obedient one, marked the dawn of the new creation, the beginning of a harmony between human beings and creation which responds to the Creator's original design. That fruitful harmony, never more critical or urgent, will go forward insofar as men and women of today let Christ's "grace" story rather than Adam's "sin" story run our world.

In the faithful witness of Oscar Romero, slain archbishop of San Salvador, in the self-sacrifice of Maximilian Kolbe at Auschwitz we find outstanding examples in our time of Pauline "obedience unto death." Alongside their witness must be placed that of countless other women and men who in our age have died or continued to live in peril of death because of their fidelity to grace. For most of us the situation is not so desperate, the demand not so extreme. But each of us in our own way can be sensitive to the Spirit's prompting of the obedience of Christ. Not for us perhaps the hail of bullets or the lonely cell. But maybe the tedium of meetings long into the night, the risk of the unpopular, unconventional public stance, the labor of persuasion — all that must go into getting things done, changing attitudes in a democratic society.

That such "worldly" activity should have its place in a spirituality for our time is a faithful reflection of Paul — something which stems directly from his vision of Christ and

God. It is remarkable that of all the New Testament writers it is Paul, the one who never knew the Lord in the flesh, who speaks most passionately, most vividly of Jesus' living presence in Christian life (Gal 2:20; 2 Cor 5:14-15). The most personal statement comes in a simple, blunt summary for the Philippians: "For me to live is Christ" (1:21). Just that and nothing more! Yet, as I have tried to show in this book, behind this terse phrase stands a whole sense of Jesus as the faithfulness of God, summoning all to obedient responsibility for "the body" and the world. Today both believer and non-believer are concerned for the "inheritance of the earth" — though only the former will see it strictly as both gift and demand of God. I trust it is now clear how powerfully Paul's vision underpins that shared concern.

FURTHER READING IN PAUL

Barrett, C.K. *From First Adam to Last.* London: Black, 1962 — *a seminal, popular survey of key themes in Paul.*

Bornkamm, G. *Paul.* London, etc.: Hodder & Stoughton, 1971 — *classic popular monograph on Paul from the German Bultmannian School.*

Byrne, Brendan *Reckoning with Romans.* Good News Studies 18, Wilmington, DE: Glazier, 1986 — *a contemporary interpretation of Romans in simplified commentary form.*

Deidun, Thomas "Some Recent Attempts at Explaining Paul's Theology," *Way* 26/3 (1986) 230-42 — *helpful, critical survey of current trends in Pauline studies.*

Fitzmyer, J.A. *Paul and His Theology: A Brief Sketch.* 2d ed, Englewood Cliffs, NJ: Prentice Hall, 1989 — *a concise and comprehensive survey from an outstanding Catholic scholar.*

Hooker, M.D. *Pauline Pieces.* London: Epworth, 1979. Published in the USA as *A Preface to Paul.* New York: Oxford University, 1980 — *clear and stimulating popular introduction to Paul.*

Käsemann, E. *Perspectives on Paul.* Philadelphia: Fortress, 1971 — *a series of essays, polemical and demanding but immensely rewarding. See especially, "The Faith of Abraham in Romans 4," pp. 79-101.*

Keck, L.E. *Paul and His Letters.* Philadelphia: Fortress, 1979 — *readable and reliable introduction to Paul from a noted American scholar.*

Murphy-O'Connor, J. *Becoming Human Together.* Good News Studies 2, 2d ed, Wilmington, DE: Glazier, 1982 — *a stimulating study of Paul's pastoral interaction with his communities, chiefly that at Corinth.*

Robinson, J.A.T. *Wrestling with Romans.* London: SCM, 1979 — *a lucid, popular companion to the study of Romans.*

Scroggs, Robin *The Last Adam.* Oxford: Blackwell, 1966 — *ground-breaking study of Paul's "Adamic" Christology.*

Trilling, W. *A Conversation with Paul.* London: SCM, 1986 — *a helpful introduction to Paul, especially for Catholics.*

Ziesler, John *Pauline Christianity.* Oxford/New York: Oxford University, 1983 — *readable and reliable survey of Paul's theology.*